Traditional
Music in
Ireland

D0931913

Traditional
Music in
Ireland

Tomás Ó Canainn

Ossian

Cover design by John Loesberg
Photography of instruments by Derek Speirs (Report)
Photograph of Tomás by John Loesberg
Special thanks to Fintan Vallely
Printed at Watermans Printers, Cork, for

OSSIAN PUBLICATIONS LTD. IRELAND
(Publishing Dept.)
P.O. Box 84, Cork

OSSIAN PUBLICATIONS SCOTLAND
9 Rosebery Crescent
Edinburgh EH12 5JP

OSSIAN PUBLICATIONS U.K
Unit 3, Prince William Rd.
Loughborough

OSSIAN PUBLICATIONS USA
RR8 Box 374
Loudon, New Hampshire
03301

OMB 48
ISBN 0 946005 73 7

To the memory of Francey and Patrick from Carnanban, John from Strone and Hugh from Kilhoyle who knew all these things a long time ago.

Contents

Plates

Preface

This is a book for those who know a little about Irish music and would like to know a little more! It is based on real traditional music, the sort that is still, thank goodness, being played throughout the country.

For me, traditional music is so much more than the sum total of all the techniques: it involves the whole person and the complete situation. The traditional musician is giving something of himself when he performs, something special that is normally hidden, and he is, I think, vulnerable in this situation. If this is so, traditional music will only flourish in an atmosphere of appreciation of what the player is doing at all levels, not just that of technique.

Some readers may like to skip Chapter 3 on a first reading, as they may consider it a little technical. It contains some interesting points, but can wait for the second reading!

Tomás Ó Canainn

Acknowledgments

I am grateful to the late Seán Ó Riada who, through his B.Mus. lectures and his friendship, made me reconsider many aspects of traditional music that I had hitherto taken for granted.

I have learned much music from my colleagues in Na Filí, Matt Cranitch and Tom Barry. The Kennedys, pipemakers of Cork, have been a continuing source of help. Among the many people to whom I am indebted are: Peter Smith, Laurence Hutson, Diarmuid Ó Súilleabháin, Paddy Keenan, John Kelly, James Kelly, Aggie White, Charlie Lennon, Antoin Mac Gabhann, Paddy Maloney, Réamonn Ó Sé, Eilís Cranitch, Francey McPeake, the late Mícheál Ó Riabhaigh, Pilib Ó Laoghaire, Willie Clancy and Peadar Broe; Seán Ó Súilleabháin, Ann Buckley,.Br McFarland, John Maultsaid, Paddy Carlin, Seán de h-Ora, Séamus Mac Mathúna, Donncha Ó Súilleabháin, Máire Davitt, Séamus Firtéir, Mícheál Gairbhia, Muiris Ó Cuinn, Dónal Ó Cathain, Jack Shea, Seán Mac Donncha, Nioclas Tóibín, Seosamh Ó h-Eanaí, David Barry, John Walsh and the Editor of the *RTE Guide*, Ben Lennon and members of various traditional music groups in Liverpool, Manchester, Belfast and Cork. I am grateful to the National Director and staff of Comhaltas Ceoltóirí Eireann at the Cultúrlann in Dublin for assistance gladly given, to Miss Bridget Doolan, Director of the Cork School of Music, and to Professor Fleischmann, University College, Cork for their co-operation and encouragement: the enthusiasm of the students in both these institutions has been a real inspiration.

My thanks to Mella Kilbride who typed the manuscript and to my wife Helen who assisted me right through the project. Without her this book could not have been completed.

CHAPTER 1

Introduction: traditional music in Ireland

It is difficult to define and analyse the basic elements of traditional music in Ireland. Clearly, the adjective traditional implies that something in the music is being passed from one generation of performers to the next. Most of them are aware of the traditional process to some extent, and of their place in it, but would find it difficult to define what exactly they mean by traditional. Nevertheless, without any knowledge of the history of a piece of music they are able to describe it as either traditional or not on a first hearing. This implies that the music has certain features of melody, rhythm, style, structure or, perhaps, even of phrasing which put it, for them, into the traditional category. Such distinguishing features, the result of the oral process of transmission (the tradition, in other words) are discussed in Chapters 3 and 4.

Yet one must face the fact that some of the best known pieces in the traditional musician's repertoire are of fairly recent origin. They are accepted because they conform in some way to the performer's concept of what is traditional — they sound right! They have, as it were, dispensed with the years of moulding and reshaping that are a part of oral transmission and have taken their place in the living tradition. The only certainty is that if they are to remain in that tradition they will henceforth be subject to a process of continuous change.

Instrumental tradition

In an instrumental tradition where the tunes are not written down but are actually composed on the instrument itself and transmitted orally, it is clear that to a large extent they will carry something of the character of the instrument on which they were composed. The composer will automatically favour certain

1

movements and passages which are either easy on the particular instrument or are in some way typical of its use in the tradition, or may perhaps be considered uniquely a property of the particular instrument and not available on others. A discussion of style must therefore include a detailed analysis of those instruments which have been important in the tradition and on which the music is still played, for it is here that style is formed and reshaped by succeeding generations. In the Irish context this means that probably the two most important instruments in the living tradition are the uilleann pipes and the fiddle. While the harp undoubtedly influenced the tradition over a long period, it has ceased to be an important part of it for the last 200 years. In confining our attention to pipes and fiddle in this analysis we are neglecting whistle and flute which do, however, owe a lot of their stylistic devices to the pipes and may thus be considered to be under discussion in the section on uilleann pipes. Some traditional musicians will rightly point out that in disregarding the free-reed instruments such as accordion, concertina and mouth organ we are leaving out the most popular instruments in the present tradition. This is undoubtedly true, but if one is attempting to define traditional stylistic aspects of Irish music it is clear that they must be sought primarily on instruments which have helped to shape the tradition. It is the author's experience that musical shapes which lie easily under the hand on the uilleann pipes tend to be traditional shapes, while those which are easy on the accordion tend to a non-traditional or keyboard pattern. This implies, of course, that it is easier to play traditional music on a traditional instrument than on a non-traditional one and, furthermore, players of traditional instruments have a built-in protection against straying outside the tradition. Their best guide is the traditional instrument itself.

Chapter 6 contains a description of the uilleann pipes and some examples of uilleann-pipe style. The fiddle is similarly treated in Chapter 7. Possibly the most vital single stream in the Irish tradition, the so-called sean-nós (old style), is dealt with in Chapter 5.

Sean-nós

The sean-nós is a rather complex way of singing in Gaelic, confined mainly to some areas in the west and south of the country. It is unaccompanied and has a highly ornamented melodic line. All melodic traditions attach considerable importance to ornamentation, and the style of ornamentation is, in fact, one of the distinguishing features of a particular tradition. Ornamentation gives the movement between main notes a logicality and inevitability which it would not otherwise have: it smooths the musical texture and, while indispensable, its overall effect should be so subtle as to make the listener barely aware of it. Ornamentation is not confined to singing, of course, and will be an important part of any instrumental performance. Each instrument, however, tends to have its own style of ornamentation, though all of them will be influenced to some extent by the sean-nós.

Variation

In many ways the Irish tradition might be regarded as a conservative one, since the very idea of a tradition is unthinkable if one does not imply conservation of certain features of the past. Yet it need not mean that there is the positive dislike of innovation implied by the word conservative, for one finds a tendency among traditional performers to alter the material they use. The change may take the form of variation of a melody in successive verses of a song, or it may be a permanent long-term change through the process of oral transmission. Both are quite common in the Irish tradition and there is ample evidence to show that they are an essential part of it.

The traditional performer may sometimes appear to resort to the use of clichés in variation or composition – he would not see them in this light of course, but would regard them as being almost the standard building-blocks, as it were, of his art. In an entirely different tradition, Albert B. Lord's book, *Singer of Tales* (Athenaeum, New York, 1974), contains a description of a Balkan singer of epic poetry which could, with very little change, be applied to an Irish sean-nós singer:

3

The singer of tales is at once the tradition and an individual creator. His manner of composition differs from that used by a writer in that the oral poet makes no conscious effort to break the traditional phrases and incidents; he is forced by the rapidity of composition in performance to use these traditional elements. To him they are not merely necessary, however; they are also right. He seeks no others, and yet he practises great freedom in his use of them because they are themselves flexible. His art consists not so much in learning through repetition the time-worn formulas as in the ability to compose and recompose the phrases for the idea of the moment on the pattern established by the basic formulas. His traditional style also has individuality.

Freedom

The freedom that the performer enjoys in the execution of a song or air is an essential part of the Irish tradition. It is a freedom whose bounds have been established over many generations by the better performers and, significantly, by the better listeners, since it is they who decide in the long run whether new developments are acceptable or not. To someone who is not a part of it, the tradition may seem to be a narrow and restrictive set of rules, but the traditional performer does not view it in this light. He finds a personal challenge in refashioning the basic material, putting his own seal on it and expressing his musicality through it. The possibilities for varying the material to satisfy himself musically are so immense that he cannot see the tradition as being in any way restrictive.

Structure

What can one say of the structure of an Irish traditional tune? The author is not satisfied that the standard classification of tunes into their various modes is particularly helpful in analysing their basic Irishness. One is not denying their modal nature — merely indicating that such a classification does little to further our understanding of their structure or method of development. A more interesting approach, suggested by the late Seán Ó Riada, is an

4

analysis of note-frequency and this is described in Chapter 3. Two other aspects of structure dealt with here are the inflection of Irish tunes in certain circumstances and the build-up of some airs from a small number of motifs.

Style

Many musicians regard style as being one of the chief distinguishing marks of traditional performance. Style, for them, is concerned with the method of presenting the musical material and is independent of it. This is not the case in the Irish tradition, where part of a performer's style is concerned with his choice of certain musical formulas and his method of reshaping and developing them spontaneously in performance. Nuances of style are so subtle and so personal as to make any assessment of them well-nigh impossible. This impossibility is attempted in Chapter 4!

The whole process of composition and transmission within the tradition makes an interesting study. In the past, and even yet, original composition as such is not the norm. One finds old material being reworked to provide the setting for a quite new song, perhaps. The jig commonly known as 'Túirne Mháire' ('Mary's Spinning Wheel') becomes the air for the song 'An Brianach Og' ('Young O'Brien') (Figs 1.1 and 1.2).

Figure 1.1 Jig: 'Túirne Mháire' ('Mary's Spinning Wheel')

Figure 1.2 Song: 'An Brianach Og' ('Young O'Brian')

The regular time of the dance tune has been altered to fit the words of the song. This particular jig has often been used in this way, and the requirement that the tune matches the text has led eventually to a number of quite dissimilar airs.

The well known set dance 'The Blackbird', in hornpipe time, is quite clearly related to the sean-nós song 'A Spailpín, a Rúin' ('Dear Labouring Boy') (Figs 1.3 and 1.4). The song has been

Figure 1.3 Set dance: 'The Blackbird'

Figure 1.4 Song: 'A Spailpín, a Rúin ('Dear Labouring Boy')

notated without bars to emphasise the freedom and sweep of the sean-nós. This particular set dance is related to many other songs, including its very close relation, the ballad in English called 'The Blackbird'.

One can trace foreign influences in the Irish tradition, due no doubt to the movement of people to and from Ireland over many hundreds of years. The influence of Scotland and England has been of considerable importance and it is possible to find material common to all three countries in the Irish tradition. It is often difficult to establish ownership of a particular tune, though one can discover where the tune was first published. One example of an air first published outside Ireland and absorbed into the Irish tradition may be of interest. It is the tune 'Tweedside', first published in the *Orpheus Caledonius Collection* in 1733 (Fig. 1.5). It was taken into the Irish tradition and combined with a text in Irish in praise of the river Lee, to give the well known 'Abha na Laoi' ('The River Lee') (Fig. 1.6). The tune is now better known as 'Ar Eirinn ní Neosfainn Cé Hí' ('For Ireland I would not tell her Name'), with its eighteenth-century text from the Maigue school of poets from Limerick (Fig. 1.7). In this version the air, with its decorations, has been finally put into what traditional musicians of today would recognise as an acceptable Irish mould.

6

Figure 1.5 'Tweedside'

Figure 1.6 'Abha na Laoi' ('The River Lee')

It may come as a surprise to many to find that an analysis of traditional composition and transmission must include the effect of error on the tradition itself. Many a tune has been changed in transmission because a musician made a genuine mistake in learning it. This mistake, compounded in subsequent transmission, could eventually result in a whole new tune-family.

One finds, on the other hand, examples of tunes which have been consciously altered to suit different instruments. A piper

Figure 1.7 'Ar Eirinn ní Neosfainn Cé Hí' ('For Ireland I would not tell her Name')

learning a reel from a fiddler will, in most cases, change certain note-patterns to make the fingering on the chanter either easier or, perhaps, more compatible with the piping tradition. It is surprising how often the two requirements lead to the same result! A fiddler learning from a piper will alter the tune so that it lies more easily under the bow or the fingers or maybe even just to make it sound more like a fiddle tune. The transmission of an air between a singer and an instrumentalist will similarly lead to changes which make the air more acceptable to the recipient.

The collections

The various collections of Irish music have never been regarded by traditional performers as a standard against which their performance is to be measured or its correctness checked. They are no more than journalistic evidence that a particular tune exists at the date of publication. No special authority is given to one version of a tune by reason of its appearance in a collection, though a comparison of collections may yield several interesting versions of one tune. The summary of the various collections given in the next chapter indicates how long some of the more popular tunes have been in the tradition, though one must remember of course that they would normally have been a part of the tradition for a long time before publication. While it is true to say that the collections of the eighteenth and nineteenth centuries had little influence on the tradition, the situation has changed considerably in the twentieth century. Since the publication of O'Neill's *The Music of Ireland* in 1903, the process of transmission has been considerably affected both by it and by subsequent publications.

Modern influences on oral transmission

All was changed with the invention of the gramophone record. One could then have the traditional player at home and turn him on, as it were, at will. Radio came next, bringing traditional music to much wider audiences, while television, a considerable time later, showed the traditional musician in action and certainly inspired learners to imitate him.

The availability of cheap tape-recorders has meant that a traditional player's repertoire is no longer his own. His music can now be carried away from a festival or a private session to spread its influence in totally unexpected quarters — not necessarily confined to Ireland, for today's Irish traditional music recognises no national boundary. One result of this is that a particular style is no longer confined to its own region. The tremendous growth of interest in traditional music, and the involvement in it of so many performers without a traditional background, makes it more than ever necessary to try to establish what is basic to the tradition and therefore worth preserving, and what is merely of secondary importance. This book goes some way towards this goal.

The last chapter is devoted to a study of three musicians of the present generation — a sean-nós singer, a piper and a fiddler, representatives of the three most important streams in the Irish tradition. Their background and music are discussed.

All translations of Irish poems and song titles in the book are by the author, except where otherwise indicated: this also applies to the musical transcriptions.

CHAPTER 2

The collections of Irish music

A broad survey of the chief collections of Irish music is given here and attention is drawn to those tunes which are still popular in the living tradition.

It is interesting that the very first genuinely Irish tune in the collections is widely known today as the air of a famous rebel ballad, 'The Croppy Boy'. It appears in both *William Ballet's Lute Book* (Trinity College, Dublin) and in the *Fitzwilliam Virginal Book* (Cambridge) under the title 'Callino Casturame' or, in Irish, 'Cailín ó chois tSiúire mé' ('I am a girl from the banks of the Suir river'). Two seventeenth-century English collections that included some Irish tunes were Playford's *The Dancing Master*, published in mid-century, and Durfey's *Pills to Purge Melancholy*, which first appeared at the end of the century. Both were published in London.

The vast bulk of the tunes that we now regard as traditional only began to be noted down in collections of Irish music in the eighteenth century. This is not to say, of course, that they were first composed at this time. In general they were tunes that were being noted from the tradition and must have been current for some time before they were written down. In a conservative tradition such as the Irish one this period could have been a very long one indeed. At this stage it is impossible to date most Irish tunes with any certainty. We can only take the date of first publication and work from there.

The first real collection of exclusively Irish folk music was the Neales' *A Collection of the Most Celebrated Irish Tunes*, published in Dublin in 1726. As well as tunes by the harper Carolan, it contains a number which are still quite common in the tradition, for example, 'Táimse mo chodladh' ('I am asleep') and 'Thugamar féin an Samhradh linn' ('We brought the Summer with us'). It is of interest to note that many Irish tunes, including 'Táimse mo chodladh', were used in the ballad operas of the eighteenth century. Typical of these was Coffey's *The Beggar's Wedding*, produced in Dublin in 1728.

We have in the Neales' collection the first published version of 'Limerick's Lamentation', a tune which has returned to popularity among traditional musicians over the past few years. There is still some doubt about whether it is Scottish or Irish. The question is considered in some detail by Dónal O'Sullivan in 'The Bunting Collection of Irish Folk Music and Songs' (*Journal of the Irish Folk Song Society*, vols XXVIII–XXIX, 1939, VI, 32). 'The Lament for Patrick Sarsfield' is another interesting tune in this collection.

Earlier versions of the well-known songs 'Tiarna Mhuigheo' ('Lord Mayo') and 'Táimse mo chodladh' ('I am asleep') are given here and make interesting comparisons with the versions sung today. The modern set-dance 'Súisín Bán' ('White Blanket') can be found here, as well as a jig which is still played by traditional musicians.

It should be clear from the above that the publication of the Neales' *Collection of the most Celebrated Irish Tunes* was an important milestone in the history of Irish traditional music.

The next collection to appear, Wright's *Aria di Camera* (1730), took many of its Irish tunes from Neale without any acknowledgment. It also contains Scottish and Welsh airs and there are instrumental versions of some of the tunes. The version of 'Limerick's Lamentation' given here differs from Neale's.

The two volumes of airs published around 1750 and known as the *Burke Thumoth Collection* contain many interesting airs that are still well known in the tradition. The tunes are supplied with a set of variations and a bass, neither of which, from a traditional point of view, do anything for the music. Tunes from this collection, like 'Eibhlín a Rúin' ('Darling Eileen'), 'Síle Ní Ghadhra' ('Sheila Ó Gara'), 'Thugamar féin an Samhradh linn' ('We brought the Summer with us'), 'Rakes of Mallow' and 'Irish Ragg' are still very much a part of the living tradition.

There are two Lee collections, the first, published in 1774, being a collection of tunes by the piping rector from Limerick, Rev. Jackson, whose tunes are still played today. It omits some of the most popular tunes by this composer. Then in 1780 John Lee published a collection of the compositions of Carolan, the well known harper, some of which have jigs appended to them and all of which are provided with a bass.

Historical Memoirs of the Irish Bards by Walker was first published in 1786 and in an appendix to it there is a collection of 43 tunes, beginning with funeral dirges and the 'Lament for the Battle of Aughrim'. Such dirges, or cries, feature in some of the early collections and the tunes themselves, with their ornamentation and trills, are in general quite different from the main corpus of folk music in the rest of the collections.

Unlike other collections, where the Irish titles of the tunes are changed almost beyond recognition (for example, 'Tommy McCullough made Boots for me', which *sounds* like the correct Irish title 'Tá mé 'mo chodladh 'sna dúistear mé' — 'I am asleep and don't waken me'), Walker's book has all the titles correctly written down in Irish script.

His tunes include such established favourites, if we may call them that, as 'Eamonn a Chnuic' ('Edmund of the Hill') and 'Síle Ní Ghadra' ('Sheila Ó Gara'), as well as the first appearance of 'An Chúilfhionn' ('The Fair-Haired Beauty'). (It is also in *Hibernian Muse*, but Thompson acknowledges in a footnote the previous existence of Walker's publication.)

The still well known 'Gol na mBan san Ar' ('The Lament of the Women in the Battle') is a further interesting item in Walker's collection and may be compared with the similar version in Thompson's *Hibernian Muse*, which was published in 1786. The tune is here known as 'An Irish Dump', i.e., an Irish lament or sad tune. There are over a hundred tunes in this collection, prefaced by an essay on Irish music and on Carolan, quite a number of whose tunes are noted here.

The habit of giving an air followed by its jig is continued here with 'An Irish Cry' and its jig, and there are quite a number of tunes used in the ballad operas. Number 38, under the title 'Irish Air from Robin Hood' is in fact the tune that Thomas Moore used for 'The Young May Moon', while 'Irish Mad Song' turns out to be, surprisingly enough, the well known 'Believe Me' in 6/8 time. Versions of 'Tabhair domh do Lámh' ('Give me your Hand'), 'Limbrick's [sic] Lamentation', 'Lillibulero', 'Speic Seoigheach'

('The Joycean Greeting') and 'St Patrick's Day' are included and all tunes are provided with a bass.

A collection with a considerable bias towards dance music was published by Brysson in Edinburgh in 1790 under the title *A Curious Selection of Favourite Tunes with Variations*, to which is added *Fifty Favourite Irish Airs*. It contains many jigs, most of which are still in the traditional player's repertoire, for example, 'Jackson's Night Cap', 'The Irish Ragg', 'Jackson's Frolic', 'Paidín Ó Raifeartaigh' and 'The Irish Waterman' which is in fact 'The Irish Washerwoman'. The tune noted as 'Carrickfergus' is known now as 'Haste to the Wedding'.

Cooke's *Selection of Twenty-one Favourite Original Irish Airs arranged for Pianoforte, Violin or Flute* was published at 4 Sackfield Street, Dublin, in 1793. While the title is somewhat misleading, there are some interesting tunes including versions of the well known 'Port Gordon' ('Gordon's Tune'), 'Páistín Fionn' ('The Fair-haired Child'), 'Thugamar féin' ('We brought the Summer'), 'Caitlín Triall' ('Kitty Tyrell') and 'The Blackbird'. 'An Fhallaing Mhuimhneach' ('The Munster Cloak') appears as the second half of a tune called 'The Bonny Black Irish Maid'.

Edward Bunting produced his first volume, *Ancient Irish Music*, in 1796. It consists of 66 tunes collected in the main from harpers at the Belfast Harp Festival of 1792. Six of the ten harpers present were blind and they represented the last generation of a line of harpers extending back for hundreds of years in Ireland. Bunting noted their tunes at the Festival and visited some of them subsequently during a number of extended tours collecting folk music in Ireland, particularly in the north and west, but reaching far into the south at times. Bunting was one of the first collectors to realise the vital importance of the Irish words to the songs and Patrick Lynch was employed to collect these independently. Unfortunately in some cases it is very difficult to wed the words and music, due partly to the fact that Bunting and Lynch were often dealing with different versions of the same song.

Nevertheless, it is exciting for a traditional musician to realise that many of the big songs of the present living tradition were being sung at the end of the eighteenth century in a form not too different from that of today. One finds such well known songs as 'Casadh an tSúgáin' ('The Twisting of the Rope'), 'Droighneán

Donn' ('The Brown Thorn'), 'Caitlín Triall' ('Kitty Tyrell'), 'Seán Ó Duibhir a' Ghleanna' ('John O'Dwyer of the Glen') and many more in Bunting's first volume. They are in a form that is close to the present tradition, if one makes allowances for the fact that Bunting could not have captured in his notation the style and nuances of the traditional singer's performance.

Bunting's second volume (1809) shows the results of Lynch's efforts, but unfortunately his texts are loosely translated and used in many cases as the basis for what are, in effect, new songs suitable for the early nineteenth-century parlour. This was Bunting's answer to Tom Moore, who had used many of the tunes from Bunting's first volume in his *Melodies*. It is fortunate that Dónal O'Sullivan's scholarly work in matching the original texts to the tunes has repaired much of the damage. Among a number of tunes from the second volume which are still extant one may mention 'An Binsín Luachra' ('The Little Bunch of Rushes'), 'An tSean-Bhean Bhocht' ('The Poor Old Woman'), a version of 'An Ciarraíoch Mallaithe' ('The Accursed Kerryman'), 'An Garrán Buí' ('The Yellow Horse'), etc.

Bunting's third and last volume, containing 165 airs, appeared in 1840. Some of the tunes had already appeared in earlier volumes and the piano arrangements in general do not add to the tunes at all, but many tunes which traditional musicians favour today are included — 'The Foggy Dew', 'An Spailpín Fánach' ('The Wandering Labourer'), 'An Bunnán Buí' ('The Yellow Bittern'), 'Jackson's Morning Brush', 'An Maidirín Rua' ('The Little Red Fox'), 'An Súisín Bán' ('The White Blanket'), 'Bruach na Carraige Báine' ('The Brink of the White Rock').

We have summarised above the main collections of the eighteenth century, but it should be remembered that throughout the period many other publications appeared, containing one or more Irish airs, in collections which were ostensibly Scottish or English. The *Caledonian Pocket Companion*, a series published by James Oswald in London from 1745 to 1760, is one of these.

As well as these, there are a considerable number of Scottish manuscript collections containing many traditional Irish tunes. A study of these sheds light on some tunes which have entered the Irish tradition via Scotland, and other Irish tunes which made their way into the Scottish tradition and are no longer to be found among Irish musicians.

O'Farrell's *Collection of National Irish Music for the Union Pipes* and O'Farrell's *Pocket Companion for the Irish or Union Pipes* were published at the turn of the century and are important from a traditional music point of view as they were produced by a practising uilleann piper. They contain 300 tunes, ranging from simple dance tunes of Irish and Scottish origin to some of the great airs of the tradition like 'Seán Ó Duibhir a' Ghleanna' ('John O'Dwyer of the Glen'), 'Caitlín Triall' ('Kitty Tyrell'), 'Erin go Braugh' ('Ireland for Ever'), 'A Mhuirnín Dílis' ('Faithful Darling') and 'Eibhlín a Rúin' ('Eileen my Darling'). The piper of today might be surprised to find here a version of the set-dance 'The Piper through the Meadow Straying', 'Apples in Winter', 'Waterford Hornpipe', and the first full version of 'The Irish Fox Hunt'.

Possibly the most interesting part is the section in which O'Farrell discusses decorations practised in his time on the chanter. It is encouraging for present-day pipers to find that their traditional method is here shown to be the same as that practised by their colleagues 200 years ago. Pipers have always known that they were right, but it is pleasant to have it so unequivocally documented! It is perhaps a shade surprising for pipers to find that O'Farrell's pipes had only one regulator (the present-day tenor regulator) whereas uilleann pipes today have three.

After O'Farrell the collections proliferate and it would be impossible to list them all in a short survey such as this. It is worth drawing attention, however, to Holden's publication *Collection of Old Established Irish Slow and Quick Tunes*, and his *Collection of the Most Esteemed Old Irish Melodies*, as well as Mulholland's *Collection of Ancient Irish Airs*, in two volumes. Holden's work was done in Dublin and Mulholland's in Belfast, both in the first decade of the nineteenth century.

Mulholland states in his preface that the publication is the result of his own labours and that of his father, whose collecting had begun around the time of the publication of Neale's book. There are some 80 airs noted, all of them fairly standard tunes, but he makes the rather wry comment that he hopes this subject may be taken up by some literary character. So much for the musicologists!

Poets and Poetry of Munster appeared in a number of editions from 1849 onwards. Here the great songs of Munster are given with their airs, though they are written down separately. The versions of the airs are, in general, quite florid and have almost certainly been noted from instrumentalists rather than singers. In many cases the tunes abound with dynamic markings such as *f*, *mf*, *p*, *crescendo*, *diminuendo*, and one certainly cannot imagine a traditional singer performing them in this way.

Music is given for such well known songs as 'Seán Ó Duibhir a' Ghleanna', 'Bean an Fhir Rua' ('The Red-haired Man's Wife'), 'Clár Bog Déil' ('The Bog-deal Board'), 'Ar Eirinn ní Neósfainn Cé Hí' ('For Ireland I would not tell her Name'), 'Bruach na Carraige Báine' ('The Brink of the White Rock') and 'An Raibh tú ar an gCarraig?' ('Were you at Carrick?'). The last is a rather frightening example of the worst excesses of a player who feels that the more notes he puts into a tune the better it is.

Undoubtedly the next greatest collector after Bunting was Petrie, whose *Ancient Music of Ireland* was published in Dublin in 1855. It contains a total of 147 airs, with a long preface and very interesting notes on the individual tunes.

A version of 'Nancy the Pride of the East' given here is now commonly known as 'Ar Eirinn ní Neósfainn Cé Hí', while 'Ar Thaoibh na Carraige Báine' is, in fact, 'Bruach na Carraige Báine', even though in the introduction to the tune Petrie spends some time attempting to prove that the tune is not, in fact, called 'Bruach na Carraige Báine'. He has a different version of the still well known 'Bhí Bean Uasal' ('There was a Lady') with rather caustic comments on the sobriety of the individual who wrote the verse in which the Kilkenny marble is mentioned! The impression of a rather conservative author is further strengthened by Petrie's frequent references to the inadmissibility of certain texts. Referring to the tune 'Cearc agus Coileach a d'imigh le Chéile' ('A Hen and a Cock went away Together') he says, 'The Irish song to this air is also inadmissible in this work', while in discussing 'Slán le Máigh' ('Farewell to the Maigue') he speaks of its author as 'the clever but deplorably licentious Irish poet Andrew Magrath' and 'one of the most distinguished of a class of men — usually hedge schoolmasters — who, for nearly a century by their writings, teachings and, too generally, reckless lives, exercised an influence over the minds and, as may be feared, even the moral feelings of

16

the fine-hearted but excitable peasantry of Munster'!

Petrie gives here a caoine from the playing of Frank Keane, originally from County Clare and living then in Dublin. He learned it from the singing of the women of County Clare but could not remember any of the words. The tune is very much a part of the tradition today and is, in fact, the well known 'Lament for Eoghan Rua' which has now become a fiddler's showpiece. Petrie also published here for the first time an air which he obtained from Miss Jane Ross of Limavady, now known as the famous 'Londonderry Air'.

In 1877, eleven years after Petrie's death, Hoffman's arrangement of 196 tunes from the Petrie Collection appeared, along with what Hoffman calls 'specimens of the ancient Church music of Ireland', as well as three tunes from the *Fitzwilliam Virginal Book*, 'The Irish Ho-Hone', 'The Irish Dumpe' and 'Callino Castaurame'. It contains versions of 'My Wife is Sick' ('Castle of Dromore') in 6/8 time, 'Cill Chais' (noted as 'An Arran Air') and 'Caitlín Triall' (noted as 'The Little Red Lark'). It is interesting that the tune he gives as number 115 — 'An Arranmore Tune' — is yet another version of the 'Lament for Eoghan Rua', discussed above. The song that is known today as 'Bríd Og Ní Mháille' ('Young Bridie O'Malley') is given here as 'Donnel O'Daly', and a somewhat different version is given as 'I'm a Young Little Girl' ('Is Cailín Beag Og mé'), while the tune of 'Down by the Sally Gardens' is called here 'The Maids of Mourne Shore'. The arrangements by Hoffman, though simple and not overdone, share the fault that all the arrangers of the time had, namely, a tendency to make the music fit their idea of its correct outline, viewed from the harmonic standpoint of the period. It is easy for today's musicians to condemn them, but it should be remembered that neo-modal harmony was largely unknown at the time and, if simple piano arrangements had to be produced, then those of Hoffman were far from being the worst examples of folk-music arrangement available.

In 1882 a slim volume of Petrie's tunes, with his own notes, was published in Dublin by Gill, with the title *Music of Ireland*, at the attractive price of one shilling and sixpence. It contains 39 tunes with notes on each, in much the same format as his *Ancient Music of Ireland*. He refers back to the last tune in his first volume,

'As a Soldier and a Sailor were Walking One Day', and gives four further related tunes collected by Joyce. These are the tunes referred to later in Joyce's *Ancient Irish Music*. The well known 'Priosúin Chluain Meala' ('The Prison of Clonmel') is one of many traditional airs which could be added to this particular family. He gives a couple of versions of 'Seoladh na nGamhan' ('The Driving of the Calves') and shows its relationship to the well known 'Boyne Water'. The collection contains a number of dance tunes.

Stanford issued the *Complete Petrie Collection* in 1905, some forty years after Petrie's death. It had a total of 1,582 tunes, without piano arrangements and without notes on the tunes themselves. A comparison of the contents with Petrie's earlier annotated collections gives one some idea of the great loss that Irish musicology suffered in the death of Petrie. This is not to hide his faults which have been mentioned previously, but rather to demonstrate the magnitude of his achievements in the field of Irish music.

Joyce published his first volume, *Ancient Irish Music*, in 1875. It is worth remembering that Joyce was much nearer to the living tradition than any of the collectors mentioned above, with the possible exception of O'Farrell, and this is evident in his selection of tunes and in his notes to them. Many of them are from his own memory of his childhood in Glenosheen and bear the imprint of the real Irish tradition. Some, however, are of Scottish or English origin, as Joyce was not particularly selective in his choice of tunes for inclusion in the collection. He gives examples of tune-families and shows their connections, his first example being 'An Cumhain leatsa an Oíche úd?' ('Do you remember that night?') and three other tunes of the same family, all collected by him in the Limerick area.

Harmonies were supplied for the tunes by J. W. Glover, who writes in the preface: 'I have avoided all abstruse treatment as out of place; and I have merely endeavoured to give the melodies such natural harmonies as will be in accordance with their character, and at the same time will enable them to be readily caught up by the popular ear, and to be retained there.' Joyce himself discusses the tendency of most collectors to change modal tunes into minor airs, with a sharpened seventh, thereby changing their whole character. One feels that he was referring particularly to his immediate predecessor in the field, Petrie, who consistently erred in this way. Joyce himself, however, was not clear on the modal system and generally refers to tunes in the minor mode without a sharpened seventh, when he actually meant the Aeolian mode. At other times he talks about the minor mode with a sharpened sixth, when he means the Dorian mode.

It is difficult not to be shocked by the apparent disregard that Joyce had for many of the texts of the songs he collected. Writing of the famous song 'An Ciarraíoch Mallaithe' ('The Accursed Kerryman'), he says: 'Of the Irish song I retain only a few fragments, which are not worth preserving. Perhaps the reader will be better pleased if I give instead a song of my brother's, composed to suit the air.' He gives the air of 'Young Roger was a Ploughboy', but feels that the words he heard for it in his boyhood were 'not fit for publication'. Not only does he substitute a song his brother wrote for the air but even alters a few of its lines, pointing out that he had done this 'on my own responsibility, as there was no time to communicate with the author across the Atlantic'. Many other songs were maltreated in a similar fashion, but he reserved his major efforts for the last song in the collection, 'Willy Leonard'. In the introduction to his amended version he says: 'The ballad, as I received it, is a singular mixture of vigour and imbecility; in some parts vivid and true to nature, in others vulgar, feeble and prosy. I have curtailed the tedious matter-of-fact narrative at the end and retrenched other parts also; added something of my own; changed many of the lines; and restored the rhythm where it was necessary. But I have retained as much of the old ballad as possible.'

Old Irish Folk Music and Songs by Joyce was published in 1909. It contains 842 airs subdivided into four sections. The first and largest section contains tunes either noted down by Joyce himself, sent to him by others, or remembered from his childhood. This accounts for somewhat less than half of the total. The next largest section, Part III, containing just under a third of the airs, is from the Forde collection which, along with the Pigot collection, was placed at Joyce's disposal by Mrs Lyons, wife of the Dublin physician Dr Robert Lyons. A representative selection from the Pigot collection is given in Part IV and it is worth remarking that Petrie also had access to this manuscript. Part II of Joyce's book consists of 58 Anglo-Irish folk songs with words written below the notes of the tunes, and containing such popular songs as 'The Boyne Water', 'The Blackbird' ('Bonny Bunch of Roses'), 'Brennan on the Moor', 'The Colleen Rua', 'Droighneán Donn' ('The Brown Thorn' — English version), 'The Dear Irish Boy', 'The Enniskillen Dragoon', 'Willie Reilly', 'The Curragh of Kildare', etc.

One cannot leave Joyce without mentioning his *Irish Peasant Songs* and *Irish Music and Song*, the latter containing good versions of some of the best known songs in Irish, with translations by various authors including Joyce himself. It includes 'Páistín Fionn' ('The Fair-haired Child'), 'Seán Ó Duibhir a' Ghleanna' ('John O'Dwyer of the Glen'), 'Ar Eirinn ní Neósfainn Cé Hí' ('For Ireland I would not tell her Name'), 'Máire Bhéal Atha h-Amhnais' ('Mary from Ballyhaunis'), 'Bán-chnoic Eireann Ogh' ('The White Hills of Dear Ireland'), 'Gráinne Mhaol' ('Granuaile'), etc., to give a total of twenty songs.

Joyce might well be considered the link between what one could call the drier music of the earlier collectors and the modern period. A large amount of the music that he collected is still alive in the tradition, whereas a considerable portion of that published by the collectors before him has died. This applies particularly to the songs that he collected but not perhaps to the same extent to the dance music, because the person considered by traditional musicians to be the most important dance-music collector was just beginning his work. He was, of course, Francis O'Neill, whose first publication was *The Music of Ireland*, published in 1903. While academic musicians could rightly point out that many of the airs had been published previously and others were not, in fact, traditional at all, the fact remains that this collection of dance music and airs and the subsequent *Dance Music of Ireland*, published in 1907, are still an important landmark for the traditional musician. O'Neill's publications, produced in Chicago and contributed to by so many Irish immigrants in America, give some indication of the wealth of music that was largely lost to this country during the last century. While it is true that some of it persisted in its new home relatively unchanged and had an indirect effect on American folk music, the vast majority of it died with the musicians.

The Music of Ireland contains 1,850 tunes, more than half of them being dance tunes. These formed the basis for *The Dance Music of Ireland*, containing 1,001 tunes divided into jigs, reels, hornpipes, set-dances, marches, etc. A further publication by O'Neill, *Irish Music*, contains some of these tunes arranged for piano and violin. He subsequently produced *Waifs and Strays of Irish Melody*, containing 365 piano arrangements of tunes from earlier collections and manuscripts and further tunes from his Chicago colleagues, arranged by Selena O'Neill. This publication includes Scottish tunes and is somewhat of a mixed bag as the inclusion of two versions of 'Rocking the Cradle' shows. O'Neill even gives details here of how fiddlers imitated the crying of the baby:

> To bring out the tones approaching human expression the fiddle
> is lowered in pitch, and the fiddler holding a long old-fashioned
> door key firmly between the teeth lightly touched the bridge
> of his instrument with it at appropriate passages. Those expert
> in manipulation produced very amusing if not edifying results.

There are interesting footnotes with many of the examples giving, in some cases, details of other versions of the tune or its source and in other cases information on the performer from whom it was obtained.

Apart from the foregoing collections of music, O'Neill published two books. The first of these was *Irish Folk Music: a Fascinating Hobby*, published in 1910, and it contains much information of interest to the traditional musician, beginning with a discussion of O'Neill's own musical background. He has chapters dealing with the history of airs, dance tunes, alternative tune-titles and the background to his own collecting activities, mainly in America. The last chapter gives a sketchy historical account of the pipes and O'Farrell's instructions on pipe-playing are included in an appendix. Another appendix is titled 'Hints to Amateur Pipers' by the legendary piper, Patsy Tuohey. Even though the hints are in general very basic, Touhey completes his discourse as follows: 'To amateur pipers endowed with special aptitude, tireless persistence and unlimited patience, the foregoing suggestions will, it is hoped, prove both helpful and instructive.'

O'Neill's second book, *Irish Minstrels and Musicians*, published in 1913, begins with an historical account of bards, harpers and pipers. There is a chapter on 'The Development of Traditional Irish Music', with a considerable number of tune examples to show the development of hornpipes from airs or jigs and the derivation of the latter from either marches or, in some cases, reels. The largest single section of the book is devoted to biographical details of pipers from the last century and from the beginning of the twentieth century, with some information on their repertoire, pipes and style of playing. Fiddlers are discussed in the same manner, while flute players and dancers are also mentioned. Even the warpipes merit a chapter, though O'Neill has some hard things to say later in the book about the Brian Boru pipes.

A number of journals at the turn of the century published traditional music. Among these may be mentioned *The Gaelic Journal*, *An Lochrann*, and *An Claidheamh Soluis*. Many of the tunes published in the latter appeared in the Gaelic League's *Cláirseach na nGaedheal* — five slim collections which give the tunes in both staff notation and tonic solfa with some arranged for choral performance.

One of the most important Irish collections ever to appear was Martin Freeman's collection of songs from West Cork, published as numbers 23, 24 and 25 of volume 6 of the *Journal of the Folk Song Society*. The first appeared in January 1920 and the last in September 1921. The collection contains 84 songs, with the words of the first verse of each written phonetically beneath the music, and a translation of all the verses is given. There are very valuable notes with each song as well as details of the singers and their styles. All of them are from one small area around Ballyvourney and Coolea, where very many of the songs have for ever disappeared from the repertoire of the present-day singers of the area, as Lucy Broadwood predicted in her preface to the last part of the collection in 1921. Freeman's scholarly approach to his task and his determination to reproduce as nearly as he could, either by musical annotation or by written commentary on the songs, the nuances of performance, means that not only has the basic material of the tradition been saved but something of the local style as well.

Munster was well served again by the publication in 1927 of *Londubh an Chairn*, a collection of songs in Irish, mainly from the

Waterford area. The authors were Maighréad Ní Annagain, who was responsible for the Waterford songs, and Séamus Clandillon. The collection contains 75 songs and includes the 12 first issued by them in 1904. Metrical translations of all the songs are given, as well as copious notes on each. These contain details of the sources of the tunes and text and information on style. The preface includes a short discussion of sean-nós stylistic devices.

Fionán Mac Coluim's *Amhráin na nGleann* also contains Munster songs notated in tonic solfa, as were those in his earlier two books of children's songs, published in 1922 and 1924 — *Cosa Buí Arda*.

The most important collection of Munster songs is Liam de Noraidh's *Ceol o'n Mumhain* (An Clochomhar, Dublin, 1965), containing some 40 songs notes by the author while he was working for the Irish Folklore Commission. The book has an important foreword on Irish traditional music and on the style of performance of the songs. An attempt is made to notate subtle details of style such as microtonal slides and glottal stops. Notes are appended to many of the songs, giving details of the singers and the source of their tradition. No other book of Irish songs is so meticulously annotated: it is obviously the work of someone to whom the style of the music was of primary importance.

The Northern tradition influenced Herbert Hughes to produce his *Songs of Uladh* in 1904, followed by the first volume of *Irish Country Songs* in 1909. This contains a number of well known songs in English with piano accompaniment. Hardebeck, at about the same time, produced his *Seóda Ceoil*, arrangements by himself of some of the better known Gaelic songs. These books, and subsequent volumes by the same two authors, had a very marked influence, and still have, on the style of singing adopted by what one might call the concert singers of the folk-music revival movement. They are far removed from the songs published in 1927 by Father L. Ó Muirí (Muireadhach Méith) in *Amhráin Chúige Uladh*. There are some two dozen songs here, mostly collected in Irish-speaking areas of Ulster, including areas such as Omeath and Tyrone where Irish is no longer heard. Some of the songs are given in more than one version: the famous Northern song 'Séamus Mac Murchadha' ('James McMurrough'), about the eighteenth-century hero who was hanged in Armagh, is given here in three different versions,

23

two from Omeath and one from Donegal. The standard collection of Northern traditional Irish songs is Seán Ó Baoighill's *Cnuasacht de Cheoltaí Uladh* — a collection made in the Donegal Gaeltacht, mostly from the singing of Aodh Ó Duibheannaigh. There is a preface by Seán Ó Baoighill containing advice on learning the songs in a traditional manner. Even though it is thirty years since this valuable book was published, its contents, with a few exceptions, are unknown to the majority of singers in the rest of the country. It contains many of the great Northern songs such as 'An Bunnán Buí' ('The Yellow Bittern'), 'Maidin Dé Máirt' ('Tuesday Morning'), 'An Chéad Mháirt 'e Fhómhar' ('The First Tuesday in Autumn'), 'Geaftaí Bhaile Buí' ('The Gates of the Yellow Town'), 'Uir-chill a' Chreagáin' ('Creggan Churchyard'). *The Irish Song Tradition* by Seán O'Boyle contains 25 songs, mostly in English. Recent booklets by Nollaig Ó h-Urmholtaigh, *Ceolta Uladh* (Vols 1-4), contain songs from the Donegal Gaeltacht.

Amhráin Mhuighe Seola, published in 1923, is a fine collection of some 80 western songs mostly collected in Mayo and Galway by Mrs Costello. Notes are given on all the songs and variants of a number of them are noted. There are four versions of 'Caisleán Uí Néill' ('O'Neill's Castle'), three from Mayo and one from Galway, and two versions of 'An Droighneán Donn' ('The Brown Thorn'), both collected in Mayo but one of them, in fact, a Galway version. It is interesting to find these two songs alive in the tradition a full hundred years after Bunting had collected them in the same area.

The publications of the Rev. Walsh, *Fuinn na Smól, Ar gCeol Féinig* and *Sídh-cheol*, containing many songs in Irish notated in tonic solfa, were an important source of songs for schools, in particular, in the last generation. They have been replaced by Seán Og O'Tuama's series of booklets, *An Chóisir Cheoil*, containing many fine songs in Irish which come directly from the sean-nós tradition.

A collection of religious songs, *Danta Dé*, by Una Ní Ogain, was published in 1928. This was an attempt to provide a considerable range of traditional religious verse married to suitable airs, mostly traditional, from the collections of Petrie, Joyce and various other contributors, in the hope that it would form the basis of a Gaelic liturgical revival. In the event, this did not happen and *Danta Dé*, with its 90 songs, some of them very beautiful, is hardly known at all today.

Dónal O'Sullivan was a major figure in the Irish folk music world for many years, though his name is largely unknown to practising traditional musicians. His work on the Bunting collections of 1796 and 1809 means that the original words have been restored to the airs that Bunting published without words in these collections. O'Sullivan's notes on such diverse topics as Rory Dall the harper, the poet Peadar Ó Doirnín, the development of the limerick, etc. are invaluable, apart altogether from his scholarly study of Bunting's sources and his analysis of all alternative versions of Bunting's tunes. This work was published in a number of volumes of the *Journal of the Irish Folk Song Society* between 1927 and 1939. *Carolan: The Life, Times and Music of an Irish Harper* by Dónal O'Sullivan appeared in 1958 (Routledge & Kegan Paul, London). It is in two volumes, the first containing details of Carolan's life as well as all the music attributed to him. The second volume contains notes on the tunes as well as memoirs of the famous harper Arthur O'Neill. O'Sullivan's *Songs of the Irish*, published in 1960, contains examples from almost the full spectrum of Irish folk songs, including lullabies, work songs, songs of love, sorrow, drink, famous deeds, religious songs and laments. It contains many of the great songs, though traditional musicians are usually disappointed to find unusual versions of them here. The songs are all in Irish, with both metrical and literal translations into English, and valuable notes are appended to each.

Traditional players have a number of sources for their tunes apart from those already mentioned. Roche's three books, *Irish Airs, Marches and Dance Tunes*, have been somewhat overshadowed by O'Neill's books, as has Levey's *Dance Music of Ireland*, but both are very useful. A recent and very welcome addition has been Breandán Breathnach's *Ceol Rince na h-Eireann* (Vols 1 and 2), the first book in which an attempt has been made to notate traditional ornamentation. A number of tutors contain tunes, among them the uilleann-pipe tutors by Crowley and Rowsome and that for the tin whistle by Ó h-Almhain and Mac Mathúna. *Geanntraí na h-Eireann* by Ó h-Uallacháin and Titley contains many of the tunes used by Seán Ó Riada, and the *Ros na Rí Collection of Irish Traditional Music* by Ríseach and Mac Suibhne has a good selection from the standard repertoire. Tunes appear in a number of periodicals such as *Treoir* (Comhaltas

Ceoltóirí Eireann), *Ceol* (ed. Breandán Breathnach), *An t-Ultach* (Comhaltas Uladh), *An Píobaire* (Na Píobairí Uilleann) and *Eigse Ceol Tíre.*

The Dance Music of Willie Clancy by Pat Mitchell contains over 150 tunes from the playing of the famous piper. Comhaltas Ceoltóirí Eireann have issued a follow-up to their tin-whistle tutor called *Ag Déanamh Ceoil* — a collection of tunes. The Vallelys of Armagh have three books of Irish music and song for children, *Sing a Song and Play It*, as well as their *Learn to Play the Tin Whistle* series, and have recently produced a tutor for the uilleann pipes. Eamonn Jordan from Portadown, the teacher of a new generation of musicians, is the author of *Whistle and Sing*, a handbook containing notes on various instruments as well as music. Collections to extend the musician's repertoire are the *Music from Ireland* series by Bulmer and Sharpley, *The Irish Fiddler* (arranged by Hugh McDermott), *Tunes by the Hundred* by Sean Maguire, *The Rocky Road to Dublin* books by Ted Furey and *Dance Music of Ireland* by Glasgow piper Pat McNulty.

Useful song books are *Cas Ambrán* by Mícheál Ó h-Eidhin and *Ceolta Gael* by Seán Og and Manus Ó Baoill. In a different vein are Mícheál Ó Ceallacháin's translations, with music, of well known songs for children — *Beidh Ceol Againn* (Vols 1 and 2) and *Ceol na Cruinne.* Colm Ó Lochlainn's two books of *Irish Street Ballads* and Zimmerman's *Songs of Irish Rebellion* are not strictly speaking part of our subject, but are important publications. It is clearly impossible to list all the music and song settings published over the years by *An Gúm* (Government Publications), Oireachtas na Gaeilge (Gaelic League), Waltons music shop, etc.

The Irish Harp by Joan Rimmer is an historical introduction to the instrument and contains many photographs. Sheila Larchet Cuthbert's *The Irish Harp Book*, Nancy Calthorpe's *A Tribute to Carolan* and *The Calthorpe Collection*, Walton's *Irish Airs for the Harp* (arranged by Eamonn Ó Gallchóir) all contain music for the Irish harp.

The Irish Folklore Commission, over a period of many years, has amassed a wealth of traditional music: information on this collection may be obtained on application to the Director. Radio-Telefis-Eireann, too, has a large archive of traditional music.

CHAPTER 3

The structure of Irish traditional music

No serious attempt has yet been made to analyse the structure of Irish traditional music. Bunting felt that the interval of the sixth was a very significant one and considered it to be almost the hallmark of a truly Irish tune. Petrie, however, tended to concentrate his attention on tune types and their relationships, and is mostly remembered in this field for his classification of some tunes into what he termed narrative airs. Joyce followed along the general lines of Petrie's approach with, however, a readier instinct for the living tradition. Most authorities today tend to classify Irish traditional music into its various modes, correctly pointing out that the Ionian mode, corresponding to the modern major scale, is the most commonly occurring one, with the Mixolydian (soh) mode coming next and the Dorian (re) and Aeolian (lah) mode following in that order. Such an approach is much too simple and completely ignores a number of characteristic features of the music. These are dealt with in the following sections and it is hoped that they will result in a greater awareness of what is peculiarly Irish in our traditional music.

Note-frequency

There is a tendency in much of the dance music to concentrate on only a few notes of the available scale, and to return to these again and again throughout the tune. The result, far from being boring — as it could be in the hands of an inexpert player — is a tune which attains a unity of purpose and a build-up of tension eminently satisfying for both the first-class performer and the discriminating listener.

An examination of the reel 'Woman of the House' (Fig. 3.1), a popular one among traditional musicians, shows a frequent

27

Figure 3.1 Reel: 'Woman of the House'

return to the note B. In practice this would be ornamented in different ways each time, but the overall effect would be to make the listener aware of the return to a stable or home note many times throughout the performance. In general greater emphasis is given to a note which occurs in a strong position in the bar (i.e., on beats 1 and 3 in a reel in 4/4 time, or on beats 1 and 4 in a jig in 6/8 time). In this reel the note B generally occurs on such strong beats.

There are other ways of giving emphasis to particular notes in a tune. A note which is very high or very low will impress itself on the listener and thus attain greater emphasis than it would normally have, while a note proceeded to by a leap will similarly be given an extra emphasis. The first emphasised note in a tune will have more importance than later notes on strong beats, while a note which is much longer than the others must impress itself more firmly on the listener's mind.

All this leads to a method for assessing the relative importance of notes in a tune, based on the following criteria: (1) a note-frequency count giving a point for each appearance of the note; (2) the addition of a further point (a) to a note which occurs on a strong beat, (b) to the highest note on its first appearance, (c) to the lowest note on its first appearance, (d) to a note proceeded to by a leap greater than a fifth, (e) to the first stressed note, (f) to a long note (e.g., a dotted crotchet in a jig). The above scheme has been applied by the author to the well-known jig 'Cailleach an Airgid' ('The Hag with the Money') (Fig. 3.2) and leads to the following result.

The first note of the tune has its normal point, plus one for

28

Figure 3.2 Jig: 'Cailleach an Airgid' ('The Hag with the Money')

being in a stressed position and one for being the first note. The next two notes, D and C, have only the normal one point each, while the next, A, has an extra point because it is in a stressed position in the bar. The G dotted crotchet in the second bar would normally have two points due to its stressed position, but has an extra point here because of its length, giving a total of three points. The last note in the fourth bar has an extra point, as this D is the lowest note in the tune. Similarly the A in the twelfth bar has an extra point as this is the first appearance of the highest note of the tune. The note C in the seventh bar has an extra point as it is proceeded to by a leap of a sixth.

This gives the interesting result that the most important note in the tune is A, with 34 points, and the next in importance is D with 25 points. This differs from the tonality that one would deduce from an analysis of either the key signature or final note of the tune, and if one calls the most frequently occurring note the tonic and the next most frequently occurring note the dominant, one is led to conclude that this tune has complex tonality, with a tonic A and dominant D. If one defines in a similar way the sub-dominant as being the next most important note, one finds that this could be either G or E. In considering the normal tonality of tunes, one finds that the dominant is normally a fifth away from the tonic, but in tunes such as the above, which have complex tonality, such a relationship will not exist and an analysis of what might be called the more traditional dance tunes will give some surprising relationships between tonic and dominant.

The example in Fig. 3.3 gives the unexpected result of a tonic G and a dominant A. Such a situation is not unusual in the more

Figure 3.3 Tune with complex tonality

traditional tunes and emphasises what the author would regard as the melodic rather than harmonic philosophy behind their composition.

The tendency to concentrate on a certain note or notes is often influenced by the instrument on which the tune is played. On the uilleann pipes, for example, the C natural, whose pitch can be varied by the use of different fingerings, is a very attractive note for the piper because of its unique sound, and he tends to employ it often even in situations where one would expect the C sharp. Likewise, the F natural, which is normally approached from the E by a slide of the finger, will have a variable pitch and must for this reason alone attract the piper who wants to exploit the unique sounds of his chosen instrument. It will be seen later that there are other reasons for emphasising these notes but, even if there were not, the quality of the notes themselves and their position in the scale would ensure them special treatment.

A similar analysis of the fiddle, assuming that it is played in the first position, would show which notes might be emphasised and which avoided because of, perhaps, an inability to make them interesting by sliding to them or decorating them with a roll or cut.

Inflection

A note which appears in both sharpened and unsharpened forms in a tune is said to be inflected, and such inflection is common in Irish music. The first phrase of 'An Goirtín Eornan' ('The Little Field of Barley') (Fig. 3.4) is a good example of the practice.

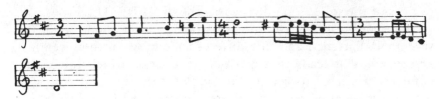

Figure 3.4 'An Goirtín Eornan' ('The Little Field of Barley')

The seventh degree of the scale, C, is natural at first and sharpened on its next appearance. The well-known song from the Kerry Gaeltacht, 'Rachadsa 'smo Cheaití bhalcaeracht' ('Kitty and I would go walking') (Fig. 3.5), is a further example of an inflected song.

Figure 3.5 'Rachadsa 'smo Cheaití bhalcaeracht'
('Kitty and I would go walking')

In the phrase 'mar a dtéann na h-éin chun suain', the seventh degree of the scale, C, is sharp for the word 'dtéann', natural for 'éin' and sharp again for 'suain'.

Inflection is quite common in dance tunes, as the reel in Fig. 3.6 shows. The seventh of the scale, F, in this case is flattened in bar 4 in the progression 5675, where the numbers denote the

Figure 3.6 Reel: 'I'm Waiting for You'

degrees of the scale – in other words the notes DEFD.

Some authorities regard tunes as being in one mode when the seventh is flattened and in a different mode when the seventh is sharpened. This leads to a method of analysis which leaves one completely unable to accept the fact of inflection and deal with it in a simple way. Irish tunes rarely change mode and to base a method of analysis on the assumption that they do seems foolish. It is somewhat better than the attitude adopted by those who assume that it is all something of a mystery!

The author has examined a considerable number of tunes with a view to establishing whether general rules for inflection exist, though it must be said first that only a relatively small number of tunes are inflected. If one examines *Irish Country Songs* by Herbert Hughes – a collection carefully and meticulously noted down by a competent musician – one finds that approximately 15 per cent of the total are inflected. This is fairly typical of other collections.

Figure 3.7 'The Verdant Braes of Screen'

'The Verdant Braes of Screen' (Fig. 3.7) shows the seventh flattened in an 875 progression. Other examples, however, show the seventh normally left sharp in this progression from the tonic note down to the dominant via the seventh. In this example the seventh is always sharp when it is going to the tonic.

'The Gartan Mother's Lullaby' (Fig. 3.8) illustrates the flattening of the seventh when it is the highest note in the phrase and preceded by the sixth of the scale. This flattening in a 5675 pattern has already been noted in the reel 'I'm Waiting for You' (Fig. 3.6) and in a slightly different form in 'Rachadsa 'smo Cheaití

Figure 3.8 'The Gartan Mother's Lullaby'

bhalcaeracht'. The seventh is left sharp in progressing to the tonic and is also left sharp in this example in an 875 progression.

'Slow by the Shadows' (Fig. 3.9) shows inflection of the fourth degree of the scale, B. This seems to be dictated here, though, by the need to avoid the diminished fifth interval E-B flat and in this case B becomes B natural in this example. It is worth noting that inflection occurs here on a weak note which is not the seventh.

Figure 3.9 'Slow by the Shadows'

One may postulate the following rules governing inflection in Irish music:

1 The seventh is by far the most commonly inflected note, but the third and occasionally the fourth degree of the scale may be inflected.

2 If the inflectible note proceeds upwards by step, it is sharpened.
3 If the inflectible note is the highest note of a group, it is
generally flattened.
4 In the pattern 875 the seventh may be either flattened or
sharpened, but it is more usually sharpened.

The enthusiastic reader may like to apply the above rules to the
tune in Fig. 3.10 and produce a well-known reel with an authentic
traditional sound.

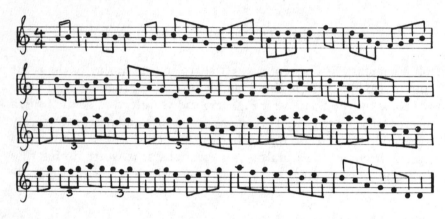

Figure 3.10 Reel

Motivic aspects of Irish music

Some Irish music displays such an apparent unity in its musical
design that one is forced to ask whether it is the result of a
conscious attempt on the part of a composer to build up a piece
of music from a short motif or is due to an unconscious musical
philosophy which dictates that development takes place by build-
ing on what already exists and letting the material expand homo-
geneously. Seán Ó Riada's analysis of the famous song 'An Raibh
tú ar an gCarraig?' ('Were you at Carrick?') (Fig. 3.11) will
illustrate the process. The opening phrase, consisting of the three
notes D C A, with A repeated, forms a motif which appears again
and again throughout the tune. Sometimes the melody, or its inversion, is used as shown in Fig. 3.12 or else, as happens more

34

Figure 3.11 'An Raibh tú ar an gCarraig?' ('Were you at Carrick?')

Figure 3.12 Motif and inversion

Figure 3.13 Rhythmic motif with different melody

frequently in this song, the rhythm of the motif may be employed to support a different melody (Fig. 3.13). The melodic motif may be transposed but is easily recognised, since it will have the same interval pattern as the original motif; in this case a major second and a minor third. The examples in Fig. 3.14 show

Figure 3.14 Melodic motif transposed

the melodic motif transposed to the notes DEG with, in the first case, the same rhythmic motif supporting it but having a different rhythmic pattern in the second example.

The effectiveness of the song 'An Raibh tú ar an gCarraig?' in performance is due in no small way to the very tight, almost austere, construction of the tune melodically and rhythmically. Such development results in a type of linear music which is essentially distinct from the more diverse and freer forms which make up the majority of Irish tunes.

The same construction is evident in a number of the show-piece airs played by pipers and fiddlers. The style is not to be confused with the kind of playing practised by performers in the last century, who overloaded all their airs with arpeggio runs which had no connection with the tune and only emphasised the fact that they were either unable or afraid to dwell on the stark beauty of the air itself. The linear approach results in music which has a clear organic growth from a basic unit or motif. Such an air is the well-known 'Lament for O'Donnell', from the playing of the late Denis Murphy (Fig. 3.15). The tune is built around the notes AGED and variations of the basic pattern, like the one in Fig. 3.16, occur frequently. One might think that the above tune would

Figure 3.15 'Lament for O'Donnell'

Figure 3.16 Motif variation

be boring in performance, but the very opposite is the case: the gradual unfolding of the slightly different patterns associated with the same basic motif results in an increase in intensity which might in some ways be compared with the build-up apparent in Scottish píobaireachd. In píobaireachd the build-up is more variational and stylised but the basic philosophy behind the two systems is the same.

A further example, this time from the uilleann pipe repertoire, is given in Fig. 3.17. It is, significantly, another lament — this time

Figure 3.17 'Lament for Staker Wallace'

for Staker Wallace, the Limerick hero. The opening phrase contains the motif on which the whole tune is constructed. This particular motif, GED, is so common in Irish music as to have become almost a cliché. The second phrase, which is merely the inversion of the original motif, has similarly become a cliché for the second phrase of such tunes. The normal pattern is to begin expanding note by note at this stage, going first to the A and then the B and gradually opening out the range of the tune, all the time keeping in touch with the original motif. An examination of the first few bars of the tune will show this development in detail. A similar opening of 'Caoineadh na dTrí Muire' ('The Lament of the Three Marys') given in Fig. 3.18 is a good example of the type. Here the opening phrase with a decoration on the E is

Figure 3.18 'Caoineadh na dTrí Muire'
('The Lament of the Three Marys')

answered by the same second phrase going eventually to A. The tune returns to the G before expanding to the B and returning to some of the notes of the original motif. Further expansion is followed by a typical run down all the previous notes of the tune. A similar pattern is observable in 'Staker Wallace', except that the final run is upwards.

Motivic development is taken a step further in a number of tunes which, as well as having a short motif on which the song is built, possesses a further larger unit which is repeated throughout the tune. The Jacobite song 'De Bharr na gCnoc' ('Over the Hills') (Fig. 3.19) is one of these.

If one postulates a motif made up of the first three notes of the song it is possible to trace it and its inversions and transpositions through the song. One finds, in addition, that the first four bars are themselves a larger motif which appears a total of six times in the song, giving it an unusual degree of unity. The air in performance has an emotional intensity far exceeding what one would expect from such a simple formula.

Figure 3.19 'De Bharr na gCnoc' ('Over the Hills')

CHAPTER 4

Style

Style in music may be concerned with performance or composition. It can mean either the manner of performance peculiar to an individual musician or, alternatively, those common features of performance which distinguish the majority of performers from a particular area. In this way one can talk of the individual style of fiddle playing of the late Denis Murphy or Michael Coleman; one might also regard Denis Murphy as having a Kerry style of playing while Michael Coleman would be considered a Sligo fiddler.

A performance of traditional music is a thing of the moment — a few short minutes filled with music that is the result of many long hours of practice, years of listening and perhaps generations of involvement in the tradition. In the past such a performance left no permanent record save in the mind of the listener. Does this mean that it is gone for ever, without trace? In the traditional music context such a thing is unthinkable. T. S. Eliot, in his essay 'Tradition and the Individual Talent' (T. S. Eliot, *Selected Essays*, Faber & Faber, London, 1932) explains what makes a writer traditional:

Tradition is a matter of much wider significance. It cannot be inherited and if you want it you must obtain it by great labour. It involves, in the first place, the historical sense which we may call nearly indispensable to anyone who would continue to be a poet beyond his twenty-fifth year; and the historical sense involves a perception, not only of the pastness of the past, but of its presence; the historical sense compels a man to write, not merely with his own generation in his bones, but with a feeling that the whole of the literature of Europe from Homer and within it the whole of the literature of his own country has a simultaneous existence and composes a simultaneous order.

This historical sense, which is a sense of the timeless as well as of the temporal, and of the timeless and of the temporal together, is what makes a writer most acutely conscious of his place in time, of his own contemporaneity.

In many ways the historical sense that Eliot sees as a prerequisite for a traditional writer may also be applied to the traditional performer. This sense of the timeless and the temporal together is very much a part of his make-up. He sees his performance in relation to that of other musicians who have gone before him, as well as in the context of the living tradition, and he often refers to this aspect of his music.

His place is among the past generations of musicians as well as among his contemporaries. His performance only has its full meaning when measured against theirs, not necessarily in a spirit of competition: their contribution, though past, is to some extent affected by his. With every performance he is, as it were, shifting the centre of gravity of the tradition towards himself, however minutely, and is re-establishing the hierarchy of performers past and present.

The very idea of a traditional style depends on such a view of the traditional performer's role, for in measuring himself against his predecessors he is, of course, being affected by them and in the process ensuring that his performance is in some general way comparable with theirs. This is the basis of traditional style. Whereas Eliot's writer cannot, he says, inherit tradition, the musician most certainly can, even though great labour is involved in its development.

Style implies a selection by the performer of certain traditional patterns or clichés of the tradition in his improvisation. His ability to select will obviously depend on what material he has at his command: a poor performer without much experience will have a small store of such material, while a top-class performer, having a wide choice, will be able to make his performance more interesting, varying his treatment of the tune in its successive repetitions. The very best performance will require a high degree of imagination as well as experience. The performer is clearly part composer as well.

Style is also concerned with the presentation of the whole

tune, including, perhaps, the re-shaping and development of the basic patterns mentioned above. It includes the individual musician's way of using his instrument or voice in performance, as well as his treatment of the melodic and rhythmic outline of the music.

Sound quality

The actual sound quality of the instrument or voice constitutes an important element of traditional style and this will be discussed in more detail in the separate chapters devoted to the uilleann pipes, fiddle and sean-nós. There is not much that one can do to change the unique sound of the uilleann pipes: basically, it depends on the type of reed and chanter used. The fiddle, an important folk instrument in many countries, is capable of a wide variety of sounds and it is possible, in many cases, to identify the origin of a folk music recording merely by listening to the tone quality of the instrument. In the Irish tradition the fiddler does not look for the sharp bright sound of the classical violinist, but generally aims at the softer tone obtained by bowing the instrument nearer to or even over the fingerboard and using a fairly loose bow. This broad generalisation covers many personal and regional styles, with an almost endless variety of tone-colour from one performer to another: there is no absolute standard. This is equally true of the tone of voice used by the sean-nós singer. Since the performance is generally an intimate one, the actual volume of sound need not be large, though the emotional intensity of some of the big songs will often encourage the singer to adopt a fuller tone than he would normally use. He has a relaxed style of singing a highly decorated line, using vocal ornamental devices which many singing teachers believe to be seriously harmful to the vocal cords. Nevertheless, a sean-nós singer's voice seems to last pretty well into old age!

The effect of instruments on style

It is to be expected that the instruments which have carried the tradition for many generations will have left their mark on it. It is possible to identify certain patterns in the music which are attributable to particular instruments.

Piping style is looked at in some detail in a later chapter, but it is worth pointing out here that some of its features stem directly from what might be considered defects of the instrument. It is not possible, for example, to repeat the lowest note of the chanter at speed since it would normally involve a cumbersome movement of the chanter up and down for each note. The piper has to resort to an artifice, keeping the chanter raised and enunciating the notes by a series of higher auxiliary notes, performed so quickly that the ear barely notices them. One thus obtains the desired repeated notes of the music, but with an interesting and intriguing piping difference. We have, in fact, just described one of the most typical features of piping style — the cran — and others are treated in Chapter 6.

One aspect of fiddle style can be understood by taking as an example a very simple reel, 'The Heather Breeze' (Fig. 4.1).

Figure 4.1 Basic version of 'The Heather Breeze'

It is clearly based on two chords with a simple cadence, though a traditional musician would not look at it in this way. The basic version would be regarded as the bare bones of the tune and if he were a piper he might begin to put flesh on those bones with a few simple decorations as shown in Fig. 4.2. A fiddler might want a

Figure 4.2 Slightly ornamented version of 'The Heather Breeze'

greater feeling of lift and movement in the tune than that given to it by these rather staid decorations. If he thinks that the last version is rather four-square he may bow it as shown in the simple fiddle version (Fig. 4.3), thus binding it together within the bar and giving it greater lift. The staccato notes on the open D string combined with the slurs across the D and A strings are surprisingly effective in practice. The auxiliary note which separates the

Figure 4.3 Simple fiddle version of 'The Heather Breeze'

repeated B notes in the last bar is obtained by a quick dart of the
third finger. This is another example of style being affected by
non-aesthetic considerations: in this case the traditional fiddler
finds that performing a D cut with his third finger gives the whole
hand more freedom to swing than he could get by taking a C on
the second finger, C being the more obvious note for cutting and
rolling in this situation. Most fiddlers, therefore, accept the ana-
tomical restriction and play the D with a nice relaxed swing of the
hand.

The above is only a beginning, a first attempt by the fiddler to
play the tune with a good fiddling style. Subsequent repetitions
might include other decorations, slides, sudden stops, subtle
holding of certain notes in a group, a drawing-out and restatement
of a phrase — a personal interpretation of what it all means to him.

Style and the collections

The irony of the situation is that in the past collectors generally
aimed to note what they regarded as the basic tune, and would
calmly ignore all the decorations and variations so carefully and
lovingly put there by the performer. As far as they were concerned
such effusions were a distraction and not a part of the correct
version of the tune. The result of such thinking would be that the
previous fiddle version of 'The Heather Breeze' would probably
have been taken down in a form not too different from what we
have called the basic version of the tune. The same fate would
have befallen the slightly ornamented version noted in Fig. 4.2 and
indeed every other version that the fiddler might produce. Style in
this context was not something to which collectors paid much
attention: they were more worried about getting the tune down
correctly, not realising that the musician had no such concept of
a unique set of notes constituting the tune.

Music and the dance

There are at the present time a number of factors tending to eliminate nuances of style in the playing of dance music in particular. Ironically, certain features which might be considered a necessary part of good fiddling may not be desirable in fiddle music which is to accompany a solo dancer. The dancer wants clear melodic shapes which do nothing more than give the main beats of the music, with an absolute minimum of ornamentation: as far as he is concerned, all decoration and ornamentation is to be done by his feet! One sometimes feels that many dancers would be just as happy using an amplified metronome to accompany them. Does this mean that real traditional music is no longer considered a suitable accompaniment for the dance from which it grew and which gave it meaning? It is certainly a fact that its primary function, in many cases, is no longer concerned with the dance.

Group playing

Playing in groups may, in certain circumstances, be detrimental to a player's individual style, as the requirements of group playing are quite different from those of solo playing. The importance that Irish traditional musicians attach to ornamentation and variation means that the music can only be fully satisfying in the context of a solo performance. Spontaneity in group playing is, of necessity, subject to the requirement that the overall sound has a certain togetherness: this tends to inhibit the adventurous performer. The long-term effect on the player who keeps turning out the same limited repertoire at concerts must be stifling. Yet it is a fact that more and more of the better players are joining groups: one might therefore wonder if it is possible to maintain good traditional style in this context. The answer, as discussed below, is a qualified yes.

All groups have their own musical goal: this influences their repertoire and general attitude to the music. If they aim for popularity and commercial success they may think it necessary to jettison a considerable amount of the tradition and replace it with a so-called 'pop' or 'folk' approach to their music. Some have done this. If, on the other hand, their first aim is to maintain a

45

traditional style, it can be achieved by ensuring that solo performances (with perhaps an unobtrusive and simple accompaniment) are a feature of all their material. The musician taking the solo part at any time must feel free to ornament and vary as he pleases, without any restriction placed on him by the accompaniment. He must lead and they must follow. Keyboard instruments, for example, and strummed guitars, with their attendant harmonic implications, will impede the free melodic line and have no place in a group which is reaching out towards a traditional goal. It seems that this goal may only be attained by traditional means, implying that the group use traditional instruments exclusively.

Ornamentation as an element of style

An important part of a performer's style is concerned with his use of ornamentation. Some employ hardly any, others use ornaments which are completely pre-planned and lack spontaneity, while the very best players are able to ornament at will, giving an imaginative and spontaneous performance. This, of course, requires a high standard of instrumental virtuosity and musicianship and these are not common. The player must have attained such a fluidity in his technique that he can ornament as he pleases, perhaps straying from the standard musical line in making variations, confident in his own ability to synchronise smoothly with the tune again when he wishes. Instrumentalists in this group are on an artistic knife-edge. They are, as it were, being pushed from one side by the requirement of giving free expression to their decorative and variational ability within the tradition and yet run the risk of not obeying the strictures of good taste and restraint appropriate to it. Only a deep awareness of the total tradition, including the sean-nós, will help the performer here. Dance music in particular is liable to decadence in this respect.

Lest it should be felt that over-ornamentation is a modern stylistic fault, one has only to look at a version of 'An Raibh tú ar an gCarraig?' ('Were you at Carrick?') published in *Poets and Poetry of Munster* in the middle of the nineteenth century (Fig. 4.4). The excesses of ornamentation in this example are repeated in many other tunes in the same collection, giving the impression that most, if not all, of the airs were noted from one performer

Figure 4.4 'An Raibh tú ar an gCarraig?' ('Were you at Carrick?')

whose chief aim seems to have been the filling-in of nearly every interval in the tune with a florid scale decoration. In the above example they obviously mar the beautiful simplicity of 'An Raibh tú ar an gCarraig?'.

Such stylistic deviations can only occur on instruments which have the range and flexibility to allow them. The fiddle, for example, is such an instrument, while the uilleann pipes is not. The fiddle gives the performer the possibility of straying from the tradition and, consequently, its greater flexibility might be considered a disadvantage. It is very easy to slide the finger both up and down the fingerboard and this fact is responsible for the excessive use of sliding indulged in by some fiddlers. Piping style is not similarly affected since sliding, particularly downwards, is not so easy on the pipes.

Traditional musicians, then, are slowly discovering in practice what artists in other fields have always known — that there is no art where there are no constraints on the artist. Without the discipline imposed on him by a traditional instrument, it is not easy for a musician to make a creative contribution to traditional music. This will be made in the excitement of a performance, when the player leaves the safety of well-worn paths in his music, venturing out into unknown and, for him, uncharted regions, finding his way along new and stimulating musical routes, and doing it all with that quality described in this chapter — traditional style.

CHAPTER 5

Sean-nós singing

It is the author's belief that no aspect of Irish music can be fully understood without a deep appreciation of sean-nós (old style) singing. It is the key which opens every lock. Without a sound knowledge of the sean-nós and a feeling for it a performer has no hope of knowing what is authentic and what is not in playing and decorating an air. In the same way, a listener who is not steeped in the sean-nós tradition will be unable fully to assess even an instrumental traditional performance of an air because the style of playing is so much affected by the implications of the language. The situation is far from hopeless for the student of sean-nós singing, however, as some — but by no means all — of the best performers are available on record; if one is not able to go to those areas where the sean-nós is still alive, one may at least get some idea of what it is all about.

What is sean-nós singing? It is a highly personal vocal art form which has been passed from generation to generation of traditional Irish singers. The number of such singers has been drastically reduced over the last hundred years with the disappearance of the Irish language from most parts of the country. The art is nowadays confined to a number of areas in the west of the country where Irish is still spoken, but even in these areas it is already losing many of its most characteristic features.

It must be emphasised that sean-nós singing is a solo art in which words and music are equally vital. The language is, of course, Irish and the sean-nós is only completely at ease, as it were, in an Irish-speaking situation where the singer and his listener are in real communication. In many instances the performer is singing of people and places known to the listener in the locality. One thinks of the song 'Cailleach an Airgid' ('The Rich Old Hag') sung in Connemara, where most of the singers would know the identity of the lady referred to in the first line, 'Sí do Mhaimeo í' ('She is your Granny') and some of them are, in fact, related to her! One is reminded of 'Anach Cuain', the famous lament for the people of the small village of Anach Cuain who were drowned in a boating tragedy in the last century and whose memory is very much alive among today's singers. Similar tragedies in Kerry, Cork, Waterford and Donegal have all given rise to songs whose words have a very personal meaning for those who sing them. 'Carraig Aonair' ('Fastnet Rock') and 'Caoineadh na Luasach' ('The Lament for the Luceys') spring to mind immediately, as well as the famous 'An Chéad Mháirt 'e Fhómhar' ('The First Tuesday of Autumn') from Rann na Feirste in Donegal. This is a powerful song of sorrow by the poet Séamus Ó Dónail for his son Pádraig, drowned while bringing back provisions in his currach across the small stretch of water separating Gaoth Dobhair from Rann na Feirste. The irony of it was that the father, Séamus, had taken the long road home, walking the few miles of land so that his son would have the relatively simple task of rowing the currach and provisions home to Rann na Feirste. Tradition says that Séamus was stunned when he heard the news and spoke to no one until he had composed his famous lament which his brother, Aodh, who was regarded as the better poet, had no hestitation in proclaiming the outstanding composition of any of the Rann na Feirste poets and one which would keep the memory of Séamus alive when all of them would be forgotten. Poor Séamus paid dearly for his fame, and the rich language of his poetry with the skilful vowel rhyming conveys his deep sorrow:

Mo mhallacht go buan fá' bhruach a' chladaigh seo thíos
Sé d'fhág d'aicme faoi ghruaim is a rinne gual dubh in aíce mo
chroí
Sé do chur ins an uaigh monuar, a d'fhág mise gan bhrí,
Gan mhisneach gan stuaim, ach mo thruaill bhocht ag imeacht
le gaoith.

My eternal curse on the brink of the strand below;
A strand of your people's sorrow; it has made my heart a black
coal
I am without purpose since you went to the grave

50

Without courage, without sense – a useless thing, blown on the
wind.

Translation cannot do justice to such poetry, nor can it do
justice to the poetry of another man whose songs provide the
Connemara sean-nós singer with at least two of the best songs in
his repertoire. The poet is Tomás Ó Casaide who lived in the first
half of the eighteenth century and wrote 'Máire Bhéal Atha
h-Amhnais' ('Mary from Ballyhaunis') and 'An Caisideach Bán'
('White-haired Cassidy'). The latter is somewhat autobiographical
as 'An Caisideach Bán' was the name by which he was generally
known. He regarded himself as being from both Ulster and
Connacht and one finds versions of his 'Máire Bhéal Atha
h-Amhnais' sung in both provinces. He shares the fate of Séamus
Ó Dónail in being an almost unknown figure to the majority of
present-day singers, but the similarity ends there, for while Séamus
remained very much a local Rann na Feirste poet, Tomás Ó
Casaide travelled not only Ireland and England, but Europe as
well. He tells us in his autobiography that he had been a monk in
a monastery (probably Ballyhaunis) but had been expelled, either
for some irregularity in a marriage ceremony that he performed,
or because of an affair of the heart. He went to Europe and
became a soldier in a number of continental armies, deserting
when he had had enough. He was in Poland in 1733 as a trooper
in the French army fighting the Russians over the succession to
the throne there, but he soon deserted and made his way back to
Ireland via England. He failed to get reinstatement in the
monastery and began the life of a roving poet, singer and
composer all over Ireland, singing his songs to those who would
listen.

> Ar a dhul na chuain domh is mé bhi go h-uaibhreach,
> Tinn lag buartha im intinn;
> Bhi me 'féachaint uaim ar a spéir aduaidh
> Sí ag éalú uaim ina trealltaí.
> Ach faraor géar géar, smé an ceann gan chéill,
> Níor ghlac mé comhairle mo mháithrín féin,
> Is gur dhúirt sí liom tríd chomhrá grinn
> Go Béal a h-Amhnais na triall ann.

Ba mhór a thug mé grá do mo chúilfhionn bán
An lá breá ar chúl a'gharraí,
Sdo do bhéilín tláith mar chubhar na trá
Sdo do ghrua comh dearg leis na caorthainn.
Chuir mé lámh ar an chuan 'sbhí mo chroí lán gruaim
Ag ceiliúr caoin na n-éanlaith,
Snach trua gan mise ag éalú leat
Faoi rópaí is seoltaí séidte.

Oro 'chuid sa rúin nach ngluaisfeá ar siúl
Go tír na long as Eirinn:
Níl tuirse croí ná tinneas cinn
Nach leigheasfaí ann gan amhras.
Nó ba tú mo rogha inniu is inné
Agus coinnigh agat féin ón bhás mé,
Nó gan grásta Dé ní mhairfidh mé
Ar a tsráid seo i mBéal Atha h-Amhnais.

Going down to the harbour I was sad and weary,
Looking at the Northern sky receding from me.
Am I not the foolish man who did not take my mother's advice
When she told me wisely not to go to Ballyhaunis.

What love I gave you that day in the garden,
Your beautiful mouth pure as sea-foam, and your cheek like the
rowan berry.
I put my hand on the quay, my heart full of sorrow, listening to
the bird song —
What a pity you and I are not speeding away full-sail together.

Come away darling to the land of ships, away from Ireland.
There is no pain of heart or head that won't be cured there.
My own love, keep me from death —
Without God's grace there is no life for me here in Ballyhaunis.

They must have listened to him, for that song is still a part of
the living tradition in both Ulster and Connacht, as is his 'An
Caisideach Bán' ('White-haired Cassidy'). The following verse from
it is almost Tomás's confession:

'S bhí mé igcoláiste go ham mo bhearrtha
Agus ins an ardscoil ar feadh chúig mblian,
Nó go bhfuair mé oideachas agus comhairle ón Eaglais
Ach faraor cráite, a bhris mé thríd.
Is rí-mhór m'fhaitíos roimh Rí na nGrásta
Nach bhfuil sé i ndán dom go dtiocfad saor,
Mar is mó mo pheaca na leath Chruach Phádraig
I ngeall ar an ghrá thug mé dho iníon maoir.

At school until my manhood,
Then five long years in college spent,
With Church's training and advice —
Only to break through all their bonds.
And now I fear the King of Grace —
I cannot see how I'll survive:
My sins are greater than half Croke Patrick,
Through love for the daughter of a prince.

The sean-nós tradition is full of such personal statements of love and misfortune. One of the most famous of the Munster songs, 'An Goirtín Eornan' ('The Little Field of Barley') deals with the subject as artistically as any from Connacht or Ulster:

Is buachaillín fíor-óg mé, go bhfóir' orm Rí na nGrás,
Thugas searc do chailín óg i dtigh an ósta le comhrá gearr.
Ní raibh hata uirthi ná húdaí ná búclaí buí déanta phrás,
Ach téip i gcluais a bróigín: Sí mo stóirín í go bhfaighidh mé
bás.

I am a young fellow, God pity me,
Who spoke of love to a lass in a hostelry.
Neither hat nor hood she wore,
But tapes in her shoes instead of buckles of brass:
My own darling she till the day I die.

It has even been suggested that 'comhrá gearr' (short conversation) in the above should be 'córiú gearr' (short dress), to give the first mini-skirted colleen in the Irish tradition!
Love-poetry and nature-poetry, probably the two most popular

forms right down the history of Irish writing, are beautifully combined in the last verse of 'An Goirtín Eornan':

Tá gaoth aneas is tóirneach agus mór-shruth fé abhainn na
                                                    Laoi
Sneachta ar na bóithre agus mór-shioc dá mheascadh tríd.
Ní dh'fhanann fuaim ag róintibh ná ceol binn ag éin ar chrainn
O dh'imigh uaim mo stóirín; sí thógfadh an ceó de'm chroí.

There is a southern wind and thunder and the river Lee is in
                                                    full flow;
Snow and ice fill all the roads and the bird in the tree is stilled;
Even the seal forbears to speak, since she who could take the
                        mist from my heart has gone away from me.

At times the nature-poetry degenerates into a recital of place-
names which meant something to the audience in the place of its
original composition but which inhibits, to some extent, the
spread of the song elsewhere. There are many instances, however,
of place-names being changed to suit new conditions and one
finds, for example, the Waterford song 'Eochaill' ('Youghal')
being changed and sung in the north as a song about Forkhill.
Similarly, the well-known Munster song 'Eamonn Mhagáine'
('Edmund McGann') sometimes deals with a lovers' meeting on the
road between Cork and Thurles. In Irish the two words Dúghlas
(Douglas) and Dúrlas (Thurles) are quite similar and the replacement of one by the other does not interrupt the metrical flow of
the line. Many of the Cork songs of this type deal with the recital
of place-names in a more light-hearted fashion and, in this area,
there is generally a greater tendency towards a humorous approach
to a number of the traditional songs.

Do shiúlas a lán gan spás i dtosach mo shaoil,
O'n tSionainn go Rath is cois bánta Daingin an tSlé,
Ní fhacas aon áit ba bhreátha is ba dheise ná é
Ná an baile beag bán tá láimh le barra Loch Léin.

Níorbh fhada liom lá bheith spás ar Thuairín a' Chéim
Ag amharc ar an áit ba bhreátha sba dheise fé'n spéir,

Mór-thimpeall Góilín, Ath Carnán is Mucros na gcraobh,
Is ag Ros A' Chaisleáin do gnáth an ghasra thréan.

Nuair a thagann an tSamhain is geall le Nollaig acu é:
Bíonn acu gan amhras brannda mil agus céir:
An mhairt a bhíodh reamhar i dteannta an bhroc a bhíos méith,
Is an bradán ón Leamhain ag damhs' ina choire go léir.

I used to wander in my youth by Shannon and Rath and the
        plains of Daingean an tSlé
And never I saw a finer spot than the little town by Loch Léin's
          shore:

I could easily spend a day on Tuairín an Chéim,
Looking across at the finest place under the sun:
Round by Góilín, Ath Carnán and Muckross
And Ros a' Chaisleáin, where the fine lads gathered.

When November comes they treat it like December
With brandy, honey and all,
Fat meat and badgers too
And the salmon from the Laune dancing in the pot.

In some cases the humour takes the form of a mock-serious description of a series of amusing incidents, perhaps in dialogue form, with two singers involved. In most other Gaeltacht areas dialogue songs, which are quite numerous, are sung by one singer and the result is that over the years the strict separation of the verses to suit the two singers involved has disappeared. One now has an illogical amalgam of unconnected verses which are almost impossible to rearrange in a sensible order, as words and lines have been interchanged to such an extent that the original story-sequence has been lost. 'Amhrán an Tae' ('The Song of the Tea') is a Connacht song which is in the process of such change, though the dialogue betwen the man and his wife is still fairly clear:

   Tráthnóna dé Sathairn ar dhul fé don ngréin,
   Sea chonaic mé lanúin i ngárrdha leo féin,
   Bhí a bhean is í go casaoideach ag caint ar an tae,
   Is níor mhaith leis an bhfear í bheith ag trácht air.

Muise bíonn tusa i gcónaí a' cur síos ar an tae
Is an lá mbíonn sé agat ní feictear agat é.
Imigh leat is faigh tobac dom ar mhaithe leat fein
Nó roinnfidh mé leat feac na laidhe.

Is tá mise dá cheapadh gur suarach an tslí,
'Bheith ag obair dhuitse gan tada dá chionn,
Dá dtiginn isteach ag aon fhear sa tír
Is gheobhainn tobac is roinnt páighe.

Sé a n-iarrfá-sa de obair i gcaitheamh do shaoil,
Ach ag caitheamh tobac is a ligean le gaoith,
Ach taispeáin anois cá 'il do mhaith nó do mhaoin,
Is nach siamsúil an lón ag na páistí.

On Saturday eve at sunset
I saw a couple alone in a garden —
The wife complaining of lack of tea,
Which didn't please the man at all.

Sure, you're always talking about the tea,
And when you have it we don't see it.
Off with you now for my tobacco,
Or I'll give you a clout of a hook or a spade.

It seems to me a terrible shame
To be working for you with no reward.
If I were with any other man in the land
I'd get a cud of tobacco and pay.

The only work you'd ever want
Would be puffing tobacco and blowing the smoke.
Show us now where's your good or your worth.
Look at that for a dinner for children!

It is only to be expected that some of the sea disasters would
form some part of the sean-nós singer's repertoire, as almost all
the Irish-speaking areas are along the coast. 'An Ceannaí Bán'
('The Fair-haired Buyer') from Waterford is a good example of the
type:

Teacht aniar de Chionn tSáile bhí an t-arthach ag cnagadh
Do dh'éirigh an mata comh h-árd leis an tops'l
Do liúgh sé is do bhéic sé agus ghlaoigh sé ar na fearaibh
Da bhfógairt suas báite 'sdá bhfágaint sa chaise.

Chailleamar ár máistir, mo ghreidhin é go dóite
Is gur gheall sé le meidhir duinn bheith ag rinnce ar a phósadh
D'imigh an roundtop is an bowsprit a bhí taobh leí,
Agus chaillfimís an crann, muireach feabhas neart na ndaoine.

Coming round by Kinsale the ship was breaking;
The mate climbed up as high as the topsail
Calling the men and threatening them
With death by drowning in the stormy ocean.

We lost our master, my bold sea-captain,
And he'd promised us laughing we'd dance at his wedding.
The roundtop went and the bowsprit too,
And but for our strength the mast was away.

One of the most famous of all is 'Caiptín Ó Máille' ('Captain
O'Malley') from the Connemara tradition, the story of a storm at
sea, told by the captain with no lack of realism:

An fharraige gur ghéim sí agus las na tonnta tréana
O chruinnigh na spéartha agus mhéadaigh ar an gceó.
Is dá mbéadh caint ag na clára go n-inseóidís scéal cráite
A ghoireacht is chuaigh an bás dúinn is gan eadrainn ach iad.

Agus tá mo lámha stróicthe go síorraí 'tarraingt rópaí,
Tá an craiceann is an fheoil is é tarraingthe amach ón gcnámh,
Ach má's é an bás a gheall Mac Dé dhúinn cé'n mhaith a bheith
                                                    dhá shéanadh,
Ach ag gabháil go Flaitheas Dé dhúinn in aon stáid amháin.

The sea roared and the strong waves lashed.
The clouds gathered and the mist came down.
If the boat planks could speak what a story they'd tell
Of the nearness of death and how they saved us all.

My hands are torn from pulling ropes;
The skin and flesh are hauled out of the bone,
But if the Son of God has promised us death
What's the point of going against him --
Let's all go to Heaven together now.

The social history of the Irish-speaking areas is well documented
in their songs. Hunger and poverty were regular features of their
life over the last two hundred years, and this is dealt with directly
in many of their songs. 'Sail Og Rua' ('Young Red-haired Sally')
leaves us in no doubt about the situation:

Nach mise an trua Mhuire ag dul go Carraigín an Fhásaigh
Ag gol is ag garrtháil is ag déanamh bróin
Ag oiliúnt mo leinbh ar bhacán mo láimhe
'Sgan fiú an braon bainne agam a bhéarfainn dó.

Níl mé ach go tréith-lag níl maith dhá shéanadh
Agus níl mé ar aon nós ach mar an ceó.
Tá fuil mo chroí istigh dá silt, ina braonta,
Is a Dhia cén t-ionadh indiaidh mo mhíle stór.

Amn't I the pity, going to Carrigeen
Sighing and weeping — a miserable man
Cradling my child here on my breast
With no drop of milk to give to him.

I am tired and weary, there's no use denying.
There's none of me left — only a mist.
My heart is broken, my life's blood is pouring.
Is it any wonder and my true love dead.

The only alternative to death in this situation was emigration
and they went in their hundreds of thousands. One of the
tragedies for traditional music is that the songs and dance tunes
that were not buried in the paupers' graves all through the last
century were transported across the seas and lost in many cases
to the Irish tradition. It is a matter of some consolation that they
did not die completely on a foreign soil but could retain their
vitality until a later collector would find them in America,

England or Scotland: others were engulfed in a different tradition and gave it a new and pulsating life so that scholars are now trying to decide just how much of American folk music owes its particular character to long-forgotten Irish emigrant singers. A quotation from one song of emigration, 'Contae Mhuigheo' ('The County of Mayo') will convey the atmosphere of many others:

Ar an luing seo Phaidí Loingsigh sea nímse an dubhrón
Ag osnamh san oíche nó ag síor-ghol sa lá;
Mur bé síor-ól na gcartaí is an dlí a bheith ró-láidir
Ní i Santa Cruz a d'fhágainnse mo chnámha fá'n bhfód.

An uair a mhair mo cháirde ba bhreá mo chuid óir;
D'ólfainn lionn Spáinneach i gcomhluadar ban óg:
Mur bé gur dalladh m'intleacht smé i bhfad óm' mhuintir,
Dár maireann gur maith a chaoinfinnse Contae Mhuigheo.

On Patrick Lynch's boat, sorrowing I go
Sighing in the night and weeping all the day;
Only for the drink and the pressure of the law
It wouldn't be in Santa Cruz I'd lay my bones to rest.

When my friends were alive there was money to spare;
Spanish wine I'd drink in the company of the girls,
But now I am old and far from my people
Sadly I mourn my County Mayo.

It must be remembered that the sean-nós repertoire contains much that could not be said to be indigenous to the present Irish-speaking areas but has been handed down as part of the larger national tradition. The fact that it has persisted in the Gaeltacht areas is an indication that some aspect of the material, whether it be the music, some sentiment expressed in the text or even the repetition of accepted sean-nós clichés in the text or tune, allows present-day singers to identify with it. This accounts for the retention of such seventeenth-century heroes as Colonel John O'Dwyer, the brave fighter who left Waterford with a band of his followers to soldier in Spain, as many more of the Wild Geese did at the time. When news of his death was brought to Ireland 'Seán Ó

Duibhir a' Ghleanna' was composed in his honour and tells the reason for his fame:

> Eistidh liomsa sealad go neósfad díbh cé cailleadh
> Gurab é Seán Ó Duibhir a' Ghleanna is gan trácht ar a ghéim
> Go bhfuil a ghadhair, sa choin, sa chapaill go domhain fé chré
> dá gcartadh
> Is nárbh fhios cár ghaibh an t-anam bhí in árus a chléibh.

> Listen to me a while
> Till I tell you who has died —
> John O'Dwyer of the glen,
> No more talk of his game.
> His dogs and hounds and horses
> Thrown deep beneath the clay,
> And we don't know where the soul's gone
> From the haven of his breast.

In much the same way, 'Eamonn a Chnuic' ('Edmund from the Hill'), a song about Edmund Ryan, another seventeenth-century hero from Tipperary, is still sung and can be traced right back to the early eighteenth century, appearing consistently in most of the collections of Irish traditional music. The struggle of the people against repression and their participation in local skirmishes, which are elevated to famous battles in their songs, are all duly recorded in the tradition. One calls to mind 'Cath Chéim an Fhia' ('The Battle of Keimaneigh'), the story of a battle fought in the Uibh Laoire district of West Cork and immortalised by the poetess Máire Bhuí Ní Laoire.

Many of the Irish enlisted, of course, in the King's army and there are numerous references in the songs to the poor condition of those who either deserted or were discharged and left to fend for themselves, uprooted from their normal habitat and possibly wounded as well:

> Is saighdiúirín singil mé briseadh as Arm a' Rí
> Is ní fiú an dá phinginn mé thabharfainn ar chairtín dí:
> Do bhuailfinn an droma is sheinnfinn ar chláirseach bhinn,
> Is ar Churrach Chill Dara do scaras le grá mo chroí.

Is óg is dealbh gan athair a fágadh mé:
Bhí ór ag mo dhaidí is agamsa níor fhág sé é:
Thíos i gCallan do b'fhada is do b'árd mo léim,
Is beidh péire ban agam ins gach baile go seólfar mé.

I am a poor soldier discharged from the army of the King
Not worth the twopence I'd give for a quart of drink;
I'd strike the gay drum and play on the sweet-sounding harp
And I left my true love on the Curragh of sweet Kildare.

Twas young in my life I was made an orphan poor,
My daddy had gold but none of it came to me.
Down in Callan I jumped and leaped with the best
And I'll have me two wives in every town on my tour.

'An Saighdiúir Tréigthe' ('The Deserted Soldier') from the
Donegal tradition is typical of a number of songs in which the
soldier regrets the fact that he ever joined the army and hopes that
his self-inflicted wound will either prove his love or leave him unsuitable for army service:

> Nuair a d'éirigh mé ar maidin dia Céadaoin
> Níor choisreac mé m'éadán, faraor,
> Nó gur bheir mé ar an arm ba ghéire
> Agus chuir mé a bhéal le cloich líof'.
>
> Chaith mise díom mo chuid éadaigh
> Is mo chiall mhaith gur leig mé le gaoith:
> Is nuair a chuala mé iomrá ar mo chéad searc
> Steall mé an corr-mhéar ó'n alt díom.
>
> Is trua nach marbh bhí m'athair
> Nuair a chuir sé mé go h-Arm a' Rí:
> Is gurabh í an uaigh mo chrua-leaba feasta,
> Is a chéad searc nach trua leat mo luí.
>
> When I arose on Wednesday
> I didn't bless myself,
> But took the sharpest knife
> And put it to the grinding stone.

When I heard about my darling
I threw off my clothes —
Let my senses to the wind,
Cut a finger from my hand.

Why did my father not die
Rather than enlist me, his son?
There's nothing here but death.
My true love, pity my plight.

The Irish approach to religion and its implications in everyday living, if one is to judge from the evidence of songs, is a curious mixture. On the one hand there is the devil-may-care attitude which rejects all strictures and is guided by the senses alone, while on the other we have some of the most deeply religious and fervent songs dealing with the central themes of Christianity and relating them to the normal life-style of the people. Somewhere between these one finds an awareness of the implications of Christianity for everyday living, coupled with a firm determination to forget these implications when they interfere with the progress of love.

The extent of love is here demonstrated by a willingness to place God or His mother below the object of one's affections. The theme is fairly common in Catholic countries and a well-known Spanish jota from Aragon puts it this way:

Dile que no entro a verla
Que me da verguenza decirle
Que te quiero mas que a ella
Que te quiero mas que a ella.

Here the man instructs his love to visit the Church and tell the Virgin that he is ashamed to come and see her because his love for the girl exceeds even that he has for the Virgin.

Tell her I do not come to see her
Because I am ashamed to let her know
That I love you more than her
That I love you more than her.

In 'Dónal Og' ('Young Donald') the girl who has been deserted by her lover says bitterly:

> Do bhainís soir díom, is do bhainís siar dhíom
> Do bhainís romham is do bhainís im dhiaidh dhíom
> Do bhainís gealach is do bhainís grian díom
> 'sis ró-mhór m'eagla gur bhainis Dia dhíom.

> You took from me all I had
> Right and left, back and front
> You took the moon and you took the sun,
> And I greatly fear you took God as well.

In 'Una Bhan' ('White-haired Una') the lover says: 'A Una, is tú chuaidh go dlúth idir mé is Dia' ('Una, you have gone firmly between God and me').

In a Donegal song one finds a somewhat similar sentiment — 'Agus dúthaigh Dé dá gcaillinn go bpógfainn-se do bhéal' ('Even if I were to lose heaven itself I still would kiss your lips'). In Cork the situation is more complicated, the following lines being spoken by the priest in love!

> Ar maidin dia Domhnaigh agus fonn orm chun Aifrinn
> Cuirim orm an léine agus an éideadh bhreá bheannaithe.
> Nuair a chím chugham an chúilfhionn luím súil uirthi i
> nganfhios dóibh,
> Is ní ar Muire a bhím ag cuimhneamh ach ar bhrídeach na
> malarosc.

> Sé mo léan gan mé sínte leat síos go dtí amáireach
> I mbaillín beag uaigneach is gan a thuairisc ag do mháithrín.
> Do shínfinnse síos le dian-díogras grá dhuit
> Agus mara mbeadh an éididh ní thréigfinn go brách tú.

> On Sunday morning preparing for Mass
> I put on the robes and the blessed vestments.
> When I see my darling I watch her unknown to them:
> It's not Mary I think of but my dark-eyed maiden.

What a pity I can't lie with you till to-morrow
In some remote place that your mother wouldn't find.
I would stretch out beside you overpowered with love,
And but for my vestments I never would leave you.

The moral dilemma is evident in the Cork dialogue song
'Snaidhm an Ghrá' ('The Love Knot'), where the lover prefers his
love to God himself and the twelve apostles and responds to the
lady's admonition to pray by telling her that even if he were to die
he would still return to lie between herself and her husband!

Is go deimhin a mhaoinigh níor smaoiníos masla dhuit
Ná tú bhreith liom gan cead ód' mháithrín,
I dtaobh, gan amhras, gurbh fheárr liom agam tú
Ná an dá aspal déag 'gus ná maor an anama.

Glaoigh ar Dhia go dian chun t'anama
Is ar an Maighdean naofa sí céile is feárra dhuit
Sí thabharfaidh saor tú lá dhaortha an anama
Séan mo ghrá-se 'gus mo pháirt an fhaid a mhairfidh tú.

Ní shéanfad do ghrá-sa ná do pháirt an fhaid a mhairfidh mé,
Ná go cionn sheacht mblian tréis dul ón dtalamh dom:
Mar níor shín céile riamh ar leaba leat
Is go deimhin nuair a shínfidh, sínfead-sa eadraibh.

Believe me darling I meant you no insult
Nor would I take you without your mother's word
Even though I would rather have you
Than the twelve apostles and the Lord of my soul.

Call on the Lord, your soul's salvation
And on the Blessed Virgin, your best companion.
She will save you on the day of damnation.
Forget my love as long as you live.

I'll not deny your love as long as I live
Nor for seven long years after I die.
For no husband has yet stretched down beside you
And when he does I'll lie between you.

Many songs testify to a careless disregard for the proprieties of marriage and Seán O 'Tuama (*An Grá in Ambráin na nDaoine*, An Clochomhar, 1960) has commented on their simple approach to the problem of engagement and marriage promises. All is forgiven if the couple go to the church next day and regulate the affair: 'Early next morning we'll send for the clergyman; slán agus beannacht le buaireamh an tsaoil' (farewell to the sorrows of the world). In the Cork song 'An Saor', the wandering mason (saor) looks for shelter as night is falling. The woman of the house wants to refuse him but her daughter insists on bringing him in and making him something more than welcome!

> Is nuair a bhi am luí againn, d'ardaigh sí síos mé
> Go rúimín dhíonmhar aolmhar,
> Mar a raibh leaba chlúimh éin agus bratacha lín
> Agus cuilteanna ar dhruim a chéile.
>
> Ba ghairid gan mhoill gur dhearcas lem thaoibh
> An ainnir 'gus í ina léine:
> Is cneasta 'gus is caoin a mheallas-sa chugham í,
> Is geallaim dhíbh gur shín síos taobh liom.
>
> When bedtime came she brought me down
> To a little cosy white-washed room,
> With soft down bed and linen sheets
> And blankets piled up high.
>
> And soon when I looked wasn't she there beside me
> All her beauty in only a shirt.
> How gently and sweetly I coaxed the darling
> And believe me soon she lay down by my side.

When the man of the house returns to find his daughter and the mason on such friendly terms his anger is quelled when she tells him that they mean to regularise the proceedings by going to the priest's house: she does not forget to remind her father that her dowry is now due:

> Ach téanam síos go tigh Father Becch
> 'Gus comhairigh cruinn mo spré chugam:

65

'Gus geallaim-se dhíbh, fé cheann naoi mí
Go bpreabfaidh chugaibh síorach Shéamais.

Let's go down to Father Beech's:
Count exactly my dowry, dad,
Believe you me, in nine months' time
My Jimmy's baby I'll show to you.

The songs are generally not so explicit as 'An Saor', but hide their meaning in a number of ways. In 'An Súisín Bán' ('The White Blanket'), sometimes called 'Má Bhíonn Tú Liom' ('If You are with Me'), one is left to work out the details from the broad hint given in the first verse:

Do casadh cailín deas orm in uaigneas na dtráth
I lúib na coille glaise uair bheag roim lá
Sé freagar a thug sí 'dom go ciúin is go tláth
Tá an saol 'na gcodladh is bogaimís an súisín bán.'

At a lonely hour I met a fair lass
In the dark green wood just before dawn
She answered me ever so softly and sweetly:
'The world is asleep, let's be moving the white blanket now.'

The erotic symbolism of Irish songs can be understood within the context of folk-song symbolism in general, and they share many of the love symbols of other traditions, e.g. thyme for virginity, the breaking down of walls or breaking out of horses being associated at times with defloration, as is the 'workman' plying his trade of milling, grinding, flailing, etc. The association of the beautiful lady with dew (drúcht) is reminiscent of the Spanish association with salt: 'la sal que mi morena derrama' (the salt which my brown-haired maid spills). Not all would agree, however, that such sexual symbolism plays a significant part in the living tradition. There seems little doubt, however, that the symbolism does exist in a large number of songs but has been forgotten by generations of singers. How else does one explain the song 'Ráca Breá mo Chinn' ('My Fine Hair-comb'), ostensibly a rather inane song of a girl complaining to her mother about the loss of a comb, but in reality one full of male sexual symbols:

Maidin aoibhinn fhómhair is mé ag gabháil an róid seo thíos
Do casadh cailín óg orm a' crú a bó 'sea bhí;
Bhí gruaig a cinn mar eornain is scáil a' róis ina gnaoi;
Sé mo léan gan mé's tú pósta, a chailín óg, a chroí.

'Is maith an t-am fós é, a bhuachaill óig,' dúirt sí
'tabhair mo ráca domh-sa is blasta gheobhair do dhíol'
Chaumar go tigh an óil isteach is shuíos-sa 'smo stóirín síos:
'Glaoigh ar phuins do dhóthain is leig-se domh-sa díol.'

'Is dubhach a' bhean gach lá mé is buartha cráite bhím
Gan dúil i ngreann ná ar gháire chun go bhfaighidh mé im láimh
                                                        é 'rís
Tá gruaig mo chinn gan táthu, is gan áit agam a réiteódh í
'S cad a dhéanfad feasta, 'mháithrín, gan ráca breá mo chinn?'

Do stadas ar feadh neóiméit, ag éisteacht leo sea bhíos,
Ar leataoibh claí na teorann, is mo ráca im' póca thíos;
Do thugas dar Fia na Feóla, cé gur dhóite thíos im chroí,
Is ba mhaith an saol fadó é, dá dtagadh an gnó seo 'rís.

Going down the road on a lovely autumn morn
I met with a young girl, a milking her cow;
Shining hair like barley, the light of roses on her cheek,
What a pity we're not married, a colleen machree.

'Young man,' she said, 'there's plenty of time yet,
Just give me my comb and sweetly I'll pay you.'
We went to an alehouse and there sat us down,
'Call for your fill of punch and let me pay the score.'

'Tis I'm the sad woman every day of my life.
No more happy laughter till I handle it again.
My hair is undone and I've no way to fix it.
What can I do mother without my beautiful comb?'

I stopped for a moment just listening to them
On the far side of the fence, my comb in my pocket.
I swore to God, though my heart was burning,
What a great time we'd had, would it not come again?

Symbolism even goes so far as to have a long glass of ale represented as a tall slender lad in the song 'An Buachaill Caol Dubh' ('The Dark Slender Boy'), and many such symbolic songs can be accepted on either or both of two levels — the actual or the symbolic. One cannot accept, though, the attempt by the over-scrupulous to show that almost every love song is in reality a religious song. A song like 'An Raibh tú ar an gCarraig?' ('Were you at Carrick?') could be interpreted as a symbolic song about the Mass-rock, as long as it is realised that it is first of all a love song and, in the same way, one might accept a religious interpretation of 'Caiseal Mumhan' ('Cashel of Munster') provided always that it is made quite clear that it is a wonderful song of love of a man for a woman.

The drinking songs, in general, show the Irishman as a rather careless, gay character, not too well equipped to resist temptation, particularly if a beautiful lady is involved:

> Tráthnóinín Fómhair ar leataoibh a' róid
> Sea do dhearcas an óig-bhean mhómharach dheas
> Is blasta 'sis cóir do labhair a beól
> Téigí ag ól agus díolfad-sa as.
>
> Bímís ag ól, ag ól, ag ól,
> Bímís ag ól is ag pógadh na mban
> Bímís ag ól is ag rinnce do cheol,
> Is nach aoibhinn an gnó bheith a bpógadh gan tart.

> On an evening in Autumn, on the side of the road
> I saw a young damsel so modest and fine
> So tasteful and right were the words from her mouth
> Go along now and drink and I'll foot the bill.
>
> Come let's be drinking, drinking, drinking
> Let's all be drinking and kissing the girls.
> Drinking, drinking and dancing to music
> Fine sport with no thirst to be kissing them all.

A similar sentiment prevails in one version of 'An Crúiscín' ('The Little Jug'):

Is fada mé ar a' mbaile seo im' chónaí ar sráid
Ag radaireacht is ag mealladh ban is ag ól dí ar chlár.
Nuair a mheasann mná an bhaile seo mo phócaí a bheith lán
Is amhlaidh bhíonn an t-aingcís eadrainn, is faraor atá!
Is faghaim arís an crúiscín is bíodh sé lán!

Long have I dwelt on a street in this town
Courting the girls and drinking at the bar.
When the women here think that my pockets are full
It's then we are squabbling and fighting, alas!
Another jug, barman, and fill her right up to the top!

Another version of 'An Crúiscín Lán' ('The Full Jug') is a stirring call to join battle with the old enemy as fresh forces are coming from across the seas to help in the struggle. It is one of a number of interesting 'treason' songs which have a well-known chorus on a relatively harmless topic such as drinking or love, while the real message of the song, generally one of revolution, is contained in the verse. Thus the casual listener who had little Irish would be beguiled by the chorus while the natives would revel in the stirring message of revolt in all the verses.

A éigse Fódhla dlúthaigí
Lem thaobh isteach bhur dtrúpaí
Is éistigí liom go súch síoch sámh,
Go léifead startha ciúine díbh
I nGaeilge bhlasta bhoig bhinn:
Is go nglaofad ar mo chrúiscín, lán lán lán!
Is go nglaofad ar mo chrúiscín lán!
Olfaimíd an crúiscín
Sláinte geal mo mhuirnín
A bhfuil ag taisteal chugainn thar taoide, slán, slán, slán!

Come together men of Ireland
Walk behind me now as troopers
And listen to the story I've to tell.
I'm calling out my order,
I'm calling for a jug,
I'm calling for a jug that's brimming full.

> Let's all be drinking from the jug:
> My darling here's your health,
> And the health of all our troops from o'er the sea.

The well-known 'Táimse mo chodladh is ná dúistear mé' ('I am asleep and don't waken me') is another treason song of the same type where the singer dreams of a situation where his enemies will be broken down and eventually become his slaves, even pulling the plough and sowing the seed for him. The final line which gives the song its name has been known for hundreds of years in both Ireland and Scotland.

One more example will suffice to complete this short survey of drinking songs in the sean-nós tradition — 'Aréir is mé ar mo Bhogadail' ('Last night as I was wandering'):

> 'Sdo tháinig bean ó Chorcaigh chugam is do thug sí giní óir dom
> D'fhonn bheith seal 'na cuideachtain do rugas go tigh an óil í
> Sní túisce líon sí gloine chugam ná tháinig bean ó Eochaill
> Bhí jacket, hoop is hat uirthi agus airgead in a pócaibh.
>
> Do tháinig bean ó Shasana sis greanta bhíodar a' cóistí
> Bhí braisléad geal den airgead aici casta féna scórnaigh
> Do labhair sí liom den chomhrá chiúin 'A thaiscidh ghil sa
>   stóirín
> Cé againn bean do b'fheárra leat ar leabaidh nó le pósadh?'
>
> Do thugas uirthi freagra go tapaidh do réir mo dhóchais
> Go dtabhairfinn-se uain a mhuilinn do gach duine mar ba chóir
>   dóibh.
> 'Leigse a rúin ded chomhrá liom agus scaoil abhaile lem ghnó mé
> Is go bhfuilim ró-fhada as m'aithne lem eachraibh is lem
>   chóistibh.'

> A woman came to me from Cork, put a golden guinea in my
>   hand.
> I took her to a tavern then to keep her company a while.
> No sooner had she filled my glass than a dame from Youghal
>   came up to us
> With plenty of money in her pockets and wearing a jacket,
>   hoop and hat.

70

An English lady came up then, her coaches fine and polished
Around her lovely neck she wore a shining silver necklace.
She spoke to me with words so soft, 'My brightest treasure,
                                                    darling dear,
Which one of us would you prefer in bed with you or maybe
                                                    married?'

I answered her right quickly, and hope was in me rising,
That I would give a turn at the mill to each one as was right.
'Stop this conversation now and let me be going homeward,
For I have come a long, long way with my horses and my
                                                    coaches.'

The music of the sean-nós

Someone listening to sean-nós singing for the first ·time would
probably comment on the rather highly-ornamented melodic outline of the song and, in so doing, would pinpoint what is possibly
the most significant musical aspect of the art. Not all areas have
the same type of ornamentation — one finds a very florid line in
Connacht, contrasting with a somewhat less decorated one in the
south and, by comparison, a stark simplicity in the northern songs.

Two main types of ornamentation may be observed: (a) melismatic ornamentation; (b) intervallic ornamentation. The presence
of ornamentation might come as a surprise to a listener whose previous experience of the Irish tradition had been confined to a study
of the collections, but it should be remembered that most of the
collectors would have regarded ornamentation as non-essential
and therefore not worth noting, or else would not have noticed
it at all!

Melismatic ornamentation may consist of a group of adjacent
auxiliary notes decorating or replacing a main note of the melody
as shown in Fig. 5.1(a). The ornamentation may be reduced to a
single note leading in to the main note as in (b) or the replacement
of the main note by a pair of notes as in (c).

In intervallic ornamentation an interval between two notes may
be replaced by a different interval or, perhaps, by a series of step-
wise notes to fill in the interval as shown in Fig. 5.2.

The freedom that ‚the performer has to ornament the melody

71

(a)   *(b)*   *(c)*

Figure 5.1 Melismatic ornamentation

Figure 5.2 Intervallic ornamentation

as he thinks fit leads inevitably to the possibility of varying this ornamentation in succeeding verses of the song and thus to a style in which variation assumes considerable importance. Not only is the ornamentation changed from verse to verse, but what might be considered the basic musical material of the song may be varied as well.

Three types of variation may be identified. These are: (a) melismatic; (b) intervallic; (c) rhythmic. Examples of these are given in Fig. 5.3.

Figure 5.3 Types of variation: (a) melismatic; (b) intervallic;
(c) rhythmic

The presence of ornamentation and variation in the sean-nós singer's performance emphasises, if this were necessary, that such devices preclude any form of choral singing in the sean-nós. If this were attempted, the subtleties of ornamentation and variation would be ironed out to leave a standard version which all could sing but which would scarcely be worth the effort, particularly when compared with the subtle and artistic product of the solo singer's art.

There are a number of other musical features which are worth noting. The singer is inclined to lengthen important notes in the song and these are generally associated with important words. What one might call musical sense often takes precedence over the sense of the text, particularly when the singer is a very musical performer. It should be remembered that some traditional singers may concentrate almost all their attention on the words and one would listen in vain for a rewarding musical performance here, but the more gifted singer will often shape both words and music to fit his concept of what the song means.

A common stylistic device is the use of the glottal stop, that is, a sudden stopping of the flow of air in the throat leading to the abrupt ending of a note. While other singing disciplines would regard such a procedure as reprehensible, the sean-nós tradition, in common with the traditions of India, Spain and many others, would regard it as an essential ornamentation. The effect of the sudden stop is to emphasise either the note which has just been sung or the following one. The length of the pause following the glottal stop really decides the point of emphasis — a long pause seems to draw attention to the preceding note while a short one concentrates attention on the following note. There is no breath taken during the short pause, the glottal stop merely interrupting the flow of breath for a second or so, but a breath is normally taken during the longer pause. The use of the glottal stop is quite common in all regions where the sean-nós still survives and has even made its way into Anglo-Irish ballads in some of the areas, particularly in Cork.

One of the problems for the solo singer is to maintain a feeling of continuity in both music and text. He has no instrument to do this for him at the end of a line of the song or in between verses and so must devise ways of performing this function himself. One finds singers adjusting the phrasing of the song to give continuity; they do not pause at the end of a line but run the phrase right into the middle of the next line. This seemingly faulty method is justified by results, as the song has a natural momentum in the middle of the line and is able to carry the singer's pause, while the decision not to stop at the end of a particular line ensures a real feeling of continuity. It sometimes happens that the singer will only pause after the linking word in the text has been sung and the listener then knows that the remainder of the sentence has yet to come. His anticipation (stemming from the singer's last word, perhaps 'agus' ('and') or 'ach' ('but')) bridges the gap in the music.

Nasalisation, as practised by traditional singers, seems yet another attempt to maintain continuity musically by continuing a note at the end of a line even when there is no text to support it. It is most obvious on a vowel sound when the singer closes his lips thereby forming an 'm' sound like a kind of drone which is repeated at the end of other lines. A drone accompaniment is so natural in this music that the practice is quite acceptable and, used intelligently, adds another dimension to the performance. A sean-nós song, musically rendered, seems to the author to imply a continuous drone throughout, supporting the ornate melody line. Its appearance at line endings, then, in the form of nasalisation is quite natural. A practical advantage of nasalisation is that it gives the singer time to think about the song without losing pitch!

Speaking of pitch reminds one that there is, of course, no standard pitch in Irish music, but this poses no problem for the solo performer. One finds a tendency among many female singers to pitch their songs very high. The singers themselves are not, in general, aware of this but merely know that this is the way it should be done.

Microtonal changes in pitch are a normal part of a good traditional singer's technique and one finds in particular a tendency to slide up to an important note through an interval which may be greater or less than a semitone. The seventh degree of the scale with its varying pitch (either natural or sharp or in between the two) often figures in such sliding. One also finds examples of downward sliding though it is not so common. It is the author's experience that some of those who favour the slide have been influenced by traditional instrumentalists − particularly pipers. An example of this can be found in the singing of Seán Ac Dhonncha of Carna, influenced considerably by his piper friend the late Willie Clancy from Clare.

The voice-quality of the traditional singer is quite unlike that of the so-called 'trained' singer. He does not use vibrato nor does he employ dynamic effects. The song is allowed to speak for itself, with a minimum of artificial intrusion or histrionics on the part of the performer. One might see an analogy here with other artistic expressions of the Irish ethos.

Irish dancers are often criticised for their lack of exuberance and, in particular, for the non-involvement in the dance of any other part of their bodies except their feet. Those who expect the traditional Irish dancer to throw his arms about and shout in the style of another country just do not understand that the normal Irish artistic restraint combined with a minute attention to intricate patterns is exhibited in the dance just as surely as in the sean-nós style of singing. It is not difficult to see an analogy with traditional visual art in Ireland: the same attention to minute detail is evident, combined with a determination to let the art speak for itself unaided by any form of gimmickry. Sean-nós singing has the subtlety of all real art and does not easily yield its secrets to the casual listener: for the secrets are all of small dimension, whether they be concerned with variation, ornamentation or stylistic devices. The performer is only partly aware of them himself and is not at pains to make them obvious to the uninitiated listener. He has a kind of detachment which invites the listener to pay no attention to the performer who is, after all, only the medium by which the message is conveyed, but rather seems to ask him to concentrate his attention on what is being said and on the manner of its saying.

What is the manner of its saying? From the musical point of view one might add to what has already been said (on ornamentation, variation and other stylistic devices) that the material does not have so many distinguishing features as one might expect. It is certainly true that the double repetition of the final note of the verse is quite characteristic of Irish songs. 'An Chéad Mháirt 'e Fhómhar', the Donegal song discussed above, shows this characteristic ending very clearly (Fig. 5.4). The double repeated note ending is often modified nowadays by changing the middle note to the leading note (instead of the tonic), thus transforming and weakening the characteristic final cadence.

Many feel that the presence of either the interval of the sixth or the actual sixth note of the scale itself is a strong indication of

Figure 5.4 'An Chéad Mháirt 'e Fhómbar' ('The First Tuesday of Autumn')

the Irishness of the song. Frank Howes in *Folk Music of Britain and Beyond* (Methuen, London, 1969) says 'one can say at once that the interval of the sixth, both rising and falling, is a common feature that gives a characteristic ethos to the melodic shape', while Bunting asserts that the 'positive and emphatic presence' of the sixth degree of the scale is 'the feature which in truth distinguishes all Irish melody.' While it is easy to find Irish songs having the interval of the sixth as a prominent melodic feature (e.g., 'Im Aonar Seal', Fig. 5.5), the author cannot see that its presence is in any way characteristic of Irish melody. One is on somewhat firmer ground in discussing the presence of the actual sixth note itself in a prominent position in the melody (Fig. 5.6). 'Caitlín Triall' is a good example of a tune which exhibits this feature and is, in fact, one of the tunes used by Bunting in discussing this characteristic of Irish songs. The author would rather consider its presence in the context of the note-sequence — tonic, sixth and fifth degrees of the scale — and its inversion which, as is pointed out in the section on motivic development in Chapter 3, is a cliché of Irish music. The opening phrase of 'Caitlín Triall' outlines this melodic motif, as does 'Caoineadh na dTrí Muire' ('The Lament of the Three Marys'). It generally occurs in songs which are either deficient in the seventh degree of the scale or have a weak seventh. The author would tend to consider the presence of this motif as being a somewhat surer identifying mark than either the presence

Figure 5.5 'Im Aonar Seal' ('By Myself Alone')

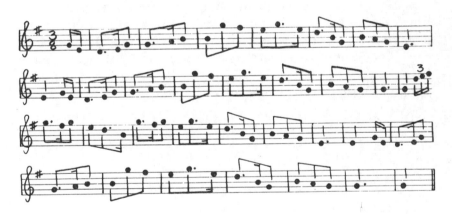

Figure 5.6 'Caitlín Triall' ('Kitty Tyrell')

of the sixth note or interval. One must agree with Frank Howes when he says of Irish tunes 'a wide range, as compared for instance with French folk-song but resembling Scottish, gives a feeling of sweep and a power of expression'.

Petrie has identified certain Irish airs in 3/4 time, having either a crotchet or a dotted quaver as the middle note of the bar — that

77

is to say, a long note in this position. He gives them the title 'narrative airs'. Joyce rightly criticises the aptness of the name but retains it in his collection and agrees with Petrie in using it to identify a particular class of airs. (Joyce unfortunately suggests a method of barring such songs which completely upsets their natural rhythm.) Whatever one may feel about the validity of this method of classifying narrative ballad airs, it has no place in a classification of sean-nós songs, as these have a freedom and variety that make them proof against any such organisation.

Sean-nós performance

Sean-nós singing depends for complete success in performance on a critical and yet sympathetic audience: it is critical to the extent that it knows what the standard of good singing is and is willing either to encourage the performer if he measures up to that standard or to make him aware of the deficiency if he does not. A good singer will feel the sympathy and encouragement of the audience right through the song, for the audience here does not feel bound to the artificial silence that is so much a part of a performance of classical music. Any particularly clever turn receives its share of vocal encouragement from the audience, and in between verses there is a regular litany of good wishes. The following list gives some typical examples:

Dia leat	God with you
Dia go deo leat	God for ever with you
Ná rabh tú tinn	May you not be sick
Nár lagaidh Dia Thú	May God not weaken you
Fáinne óir ort	A gold ring on you
Faoi do chois é	Under your foot (a dancing term)
Maith thú	Good for you
Togha fir	Choice man
Croí dhuit	Heart to you
Mo ghreidhn thú	You're my love
O Thuaidh!	Northwards! (used in Kerry only)

An Irish-speaking audience will even take part in a kind of discussion on the action of the song, making their own comments to the singer without, in general, interrupting the flow of the

78

music. He will be quite aware of what is happening and will tend to respond musically to this good-humoured banter.

The performer is generally seated among his audience since there is no question of a formal recital requiring a large volume of sound. He may be reticent and require cajoling before he will begin, but this is all regarded as part of the recital. Such reticence extends sometimes to his adopting a sitting position away from his audience and turned towards the corner of the room. This has been explained as having some ancient significance (which it may well have) but the author feels that the reasons are also concerned with acoustics. Any instrumentalist knows that the sound fed back to the performer in such a position has a most gratifying volume. It gives one the rather satisfying impression of playing in a cathedral! It is necessary, as was pointed out earlier, for the solo singer to have a feeling of continuity in his singing, and the feedback of sound from the corner of a room certainly provides this. The more usual method is to cup one hand round the ear, with the heel of the hand pointing towards the mouth. This acts as a kind of megaphone and gives the necessary feedback of sound to the singer. The singer may attain the detachment that was discussed earlier by closing his eyes during the performance, emphasising as it were that the only contact between himself and his audience is that of the song itself.

The question of contact is an interesting one because it often happens that one of the audience comes forward to hold the hand of the singer at some high point in the song and will even emphasise either the rhythm of the song or an important sentiment by grasping the hand more firmly and moving it up and down. One cannot help feeling, on such occasions, that this one person speaks for the whole audience and is conveying to the singer the sense of participation in the song that they all feel.

In the small rural communities in which it developed, the sean-nós was very much more than mere entertainment. It contained among its large repertoire the religious songs of a people who were not allowed the luxury of public devotion, their work songs and songs of love, their humorous songs and the stories of local tragedies whose horror had imprinted itself on the minds of the small community. Here too were the thinly disguised songs of rebellion, the glorification of past heroes coupled with a message

79

of hope for a new awakening, when the Prince would come from across the sea to free the people. The singer would tell, too, of the simple local happenings, perhaps adding a new dimension of fantasy to the event to provide the heroic element so necessary for an oppressed people.

In this situation the sean-nós singer was not performing, but giving expression to the shared experiences and hopes of the audience. He was not merely singing the story but attempting, by the musical means we have already discussed, to do much more. If we regard song as an expression of something which goes beyond mere words, then sean-nós singing is an expression of something which goes beyond mere singing. It might be compared with the Flamenco style of Spain. Anselmo Gonzales Climent, speaking of the seguidilla, possibly the most abstruse form of Flamenco, says that 'beyond it there is God or nothing'. The Irish might not be quite so effusive, but many would have similar feelings about sean-nós singing.

When the sean-nós singer of today speaks the last few words of the song, instead of singing them, he is telling his audience that all is over, that he is bringing us back down from the heights of our involvement in the sean-nós experience to the hard facts of everyday life. In the same way, the Kerry singer who finishes the song and says somewhat bitterly 'agus chuadar ag ól' ('and they went drinking') is bringing us back unceremoniously from what might well be called another world.

CHAPTER 6

The uilleann pipes

The uilleann pipes represent the particularly Irish contribution to the development of an instrument which has counterparts in numerous other areas of the world, notably in the countries of Europe and Africa and even as far away as India. The name used in all the early literature is 'union' pipes, but there is no doubt that traditional players nowadays call them uilleann pipes and we do well to follow their example. Some form of pipe was known to both the ancient Greeks and Romans: the historians Suetonius and Dion Chrysostom tell us Nero was able to play the pipes and we must assume that if any music was heard from the Nero homestead while Rome was burning it was much more likely to have been the music of the pipes rather than of the fiddle!

The early pipes were very simple and it was probably not until the thirteenth century that the drone came into general use to provide at first a simple continuous accompaniment and, much later, a two-note accompaniment to the chanter. The bag was inflated by a blowpipe placed in the mouth and this method lasted until the end of the seventeenth century or the beginning of the eighteenth, when a bellows was used to inflate the bag. Bellows-blown pipes exist in many other countries besides Ireland — in England and France, for instance, so that the addition of the bellows does not seem to have been a peculiarly Irish contribution to pipe development.

There are grounds for believing that the Irish mouth-blown pipes resembled the present píob-mhór or warpipes of Scotland, not only in appearance but also, perhaps, in the unusual tuning of the chanter. (The present mouth-blown pipe used in Ireland may be regarded as a revival of the Scottish instrument after the native instrument had disappeared.)

Uilleann pipes blown by bellows have a quite different chanter scale from that of the warpipes. The range of the uilleann pipes is two octaves compared with the nine notes of the warpipes (these are the normal ranges and do not take into account the extra higher notes claimed by virtuoso players in both traditions), and the actual scale is much closer to what is accepted as correct in the European tradition than is the scale of the warpipe, in which only three of its nine notes correspond with the scale based on the harmonic series. By contrast, only one note on the uilleann pipes differs considerably from this standard scale, though it should be realised that every uilleann pipe chanter is a unique hand-made product having its own tonal character.

The uilleann pipes have a milder tone than the warpipes and this is due to a much softer and more pliable double reed than the shorter and stiffer one used in the warpipes. This softer reed, besides having a mellower tone, is capable of being overblown to give the higher octave. It is not unlike the reed of the oboe.

Until the middle of the eighteenth century the uilleann pipes consisted of a chanter and two drones. At this stage a further drone was added, an octave below the other two, so that the three drones were tuned to D with an octave between each, the highest one being at the same pitch as the lowest note of the chanter. The drones had single reeds made of native woods or cane, though nowadays Spanish cane is by far the most popular material for both drone and chanter reeds. Almost at the same time as the third drone was added, the first regulator was added to the pipes. This might be regarded as a kind of keyed chanter with a closed end and a double reed quite like that of the chanter. It is used to provide an accompaniment to the main chanter melody. The regulator is generally played with the heel of the hand or the wrist, or it may sometimes be fingered with the right hand to provide a countermelody to that played by the left hand on the chanter.

What we now regard as the standard uilleann pipes, with chanter, bellows, three drones and three regulators, developed early in the nineteenth century and have not changed significantly since then, though one finds examples of pipes with four regulators, the fourth one being pitched below the bass regulator. The more normal set-up is that of a tenor regulator having five keys from F sharp up to C in the treble clef, a baritone for D to A in the same clef, and a large bass regulator giving four notes, G to C, an octave below the tenor regulator.

The regulators may be tuned either by moving the reed up and down or by adjusting a rush connected to a tuning bead at the closed end of the regulator. Movement of the rush into the regulator flattens the lower notes but may change their quality somewhat. The chanter may be tuned in a similar fashion. Opening the double reed of the chanter or regulator will flatten the top notes. The drone reeds, too, may be pushed further into the drone to sharpen it or, more usually, one part of the drone slides to give a variable drone length for tuning. Such a sliding arrangement has been suggested for the regulators but, in practice, only the bass regulator employs such a system.

It comes as something of a surprise to realise that the extended harmonic section of the pipes (that is, the set of regulators) is what is generally regarded as the most significant Irish contribution to pipe development. The irony of it is that the extra regulators were added to provide a harmonic accompaniment which would satisfy nineteenth-century ears and they are, in general, an unsuitable accompaniment for the highly sophisticated melodic tradition that we associate with uilleann pipes. We shall see that the most significant Irish contribution to piping is in the style of the music itself and in the exploitation by a good piper of what is acknowledged to be one of the most flexible instruments of the world pipe family.

Piping style

Styles of pipe-playing are influenced to a very large extent by the feasibility or otherwise of completely stopping the sound between successive notes. If this cannot be done, then various ways of articulating notes, staccato playing and the playing of repeated notes must be devised. In general, notes will be separated by very short gracings or cuts which have no musical value in themselves but merely separate the main notes from each other to give an impression of staccato playing. In Scottish pipe music such devices have proliferated and a very highly formalised system of piping has been built around them. The situation is different with the uilleann pipes as the chanter is completely stopped when it is placed on the piper's knee with the fingers covering all holes, and the necessity for an elaborate system of gracing is not so pressing. Nevertheless, when the bottom note of the chanter is sounded the chanter must be lifted from the knee, resulting in a continuous note which must be graced from a higher note. If the piper wishes to decorate this note by making it into a triplet he is obliged to grace each one of the individual D notes, as he could not separate them at speed by awkwardly moving the chanter quickly up and down. The requirement of speed in performance means that successive grace notes must be executed with different fingers and this leads to a decoration as shown in Fig. 6.1. This device is

Figure 6.1 Jig 'Why So', illustrating cranning

known as 'cranning' and is the most characteristic ornamentation used on the uilleann pipes. In this example the grace notes are A, G and F sharp, but others are possible though not so common. A similar decoration is used on the note E, but cranning as such is not so often used on other notes on the uilleann pipes.

When the chanter is on the knee (as it may be for all the notes except low D), notes can be clearly articulated, as the sound is stopped between them. Nevertheless, when the same note is repeated at speed there must be an intervening grace note to avoid having to move the same finger or fingers twice. This is shown in the first bar of Fig. 6.2 for the note A. When a triplet is required on another note, for example, it is usually executed as shown in the subsequent bars of the example. The grace notes are D or A and the middle note of the triplet is obtained by a quick pat of

Figure 6.2 Examples of close rolls

the finger which had been raised to sound the note, thus momentarily stopping it after the second A of the triplet. This decoration depends for its effectiveness on having all the holes closed except the one which is sounding the main note. This implies a particularly important style of piping, known as close or tight piping. Its main feature is that only the minimum number of fingers is lifted from the chanter to allow the note to sound. In practice this means that either one or two fingers, not more, are lifted for each note, and the notes may therefore be stopped simply by replacing them on the chanter. It is clear then that the stopping of the note in the previous ornament by simply replacing a finger on the chanter is an easy movement and becomes part of a very fast relaxed roll, for that is what this decoration is.

It is interesting to see what happens to this decoration when the alternative style, open or loose piping, is employed. In this case, for the same finger movement we get a roll in which there is no short period of silence between notes, and when the finger is replaced momentarily on the chanter as before we get a G grace note sounding since all the lower fingers are off the chanter. This is shown in Fig. 6.3. The decoration is played so quickly, however,

Figure 6.3 Open roll

that this extra grace note, G, will not normally be heard by the average listener. What he will hear is a quite different type of playing when the open style is employed: in many ways it resembles a warpipe sound because of the continuous flow of air through the chanter.

Popping, as it is called, is a method of emphasising notes on the upper octave by lifting the chanter off the knee just as they begin to sound. As well as adding volume to the sound it results in a small gradual change of pitch as the chanter is raised. This is emphasised, of course, if the note is approached by sliding from below. This is shown in the first bar of Fig. 6.4 for the note G and its possible use in the tune 'Captain Bing'.

Since the second octave is overblown, the necessary pressure in

Figure 6.4 Use of popping in the tune 'Captain Bing'

the chanter can only be obtained from the closed position, that is with all holes shut and the chanter on the knee. In many modern chanters there is a gravity valve at the bottom of the chanter which opens automatically when the chanter is lifted but provides an air-seal when it is placed on the knee. Formerly, a piece of leather (the piper's apron) was placed on the knee to ensure an airtight junction here, as clothing would not provide this satisfactorily at the higher air pressure required for the second octave. When a note is to be popped it must first be sounded from the closed position and the chanter then lifted: the note will continue to sound since it is only the initial attack on a note in the second octave which requires the higher pressure, not the maintenance of the note itself. Some pipers feel that the use of the valve inhibits their popping style. In particular, they are of the opinion that the attack on the note is slowed down when a valve is used. This has not been the author's experience.

It is worth pointing out that not only is there a slight difference in pitch when a note is popped, but the harmonic content of the note is changed to give a quite distinctive sound much relished by pipers. Provided it is not carried to excess, this emphasis on the peculiar and distinctive sounds of the pipes is an important part of the traditional style of uilleann-pipe playing. It is further illustrated by the emphasis which a good piper puts on those notes of the chanter which have a distinctive tone quality. The bottom note of the chanter has two distinct sounds and the intelligent variation of these adds interest to the playing. The first of these notes has a smooth soft quality, whereas the second, which is produced by slightly increasing the pressure of air, is rather more strident with a hard tonal edge. For this reason pipers call it the hard D and for many of them it is the only low D worth playing. The hard D is not difficult to produce in performance, but care must be taken not to increase air pressure unduly or the chanter will overblow and give an entirely different note.

Another note with a distinctive sound and varying pitch, depending on the fingering, is the C in the lower octave — usually called the piper's C. Due to the cross-fingering required to produce it in tune, it does not normally figure as an auxiliary note but it is usually emphasised in performance. Its variable pitch may be further accentuated by a quite wide vibrato provided by the two middle fingers of the right hand. For tunes with a final D, this note is of course the seventh degree of the scale and its pitch is between the C natural and C sharp of the tempered scale. What has been said elsewhere on inflection indicates why this note is of such importance in many Irish traditional tunes. The F natural in the upper octave, being the seventh degree of the scale for tunes ending in G, is likewise of considerable importance. It is normal to obtain it by partly opening one of the holes on the chanter and in this way its pitch can be varied over quite a wide range to suit different tunes. Many pipers employ a key for this F natural, and while this may be of assistance in some dance music it means that the very flexible sliding and pitch variation obtained by using the finger is no longer available to the player. The absence of this facility is a major disadvantage in the playing of slow airs.

The piper may obtain variety in performance by playing the chanter alone at first and then introducing the drones to give depth to the music. A few pipers stop the base drone for a part of the tune and set it going later for the same reason. This should not be confused with the accidental stopping of the drone due to either a faulty reed or too great an air pressure while the chanter is playing in the second octave. Embryo pipers will be glad to hear that there is now a possibility of their faults being mistaken for stylistic devices!

It has already been pointed out that the harmonic accompaniment provided by the regulators, particularly in the hands of an insensitive player, is a very mixed blessing indeed. The layout of the keys is a direct invitation to the piper to put the heel of his hand across all three regulators and obtain block chords which tend to obscure the melody, not only because of their chordal nature but because of the lack of balance between the three regulator reeds and the single chanter reed. Many pipers do not seem to be aware of the musical satisfaction given by the interplay between a decorated melodic line and a steady drone which provides a large number of higher harmonics. Such a system is largely self-sufficient and has been the basic formula for much of the world's folk music for thousands of years. The sophisticated Indian system of a vina accompanied by a tambura provides a direct parallel with the uilleann pipes of the Irish tradition. Who would dare to say that Indian music would be the richer for the addition of a nineteenth-century chordal system to a music which was practised and analysed thousands of years before the beginning of the Christian era?

The fact remains, however, that the regulators are an integral part of the uilleann pipes and are used to a greater or lesser extent by most pipers. In dance music they are employed mainly as a rhythmic device giving either a vamping bass as shown in Fig. 6.5

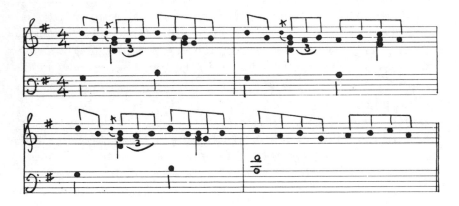

Figure 6.5 Vamping regulator accompaniment

or, occasionally, a two- or three-part chord may be held right through a bar. The vamping bass is often obtained by using the front part of the heel of the hand for the single notes on the bass regulator, while the double notes are produced by striking the baritone and tenor regulator keys simultaneously with the heel of the hand or wrist. When playing at speed this results in a rocking action of the hand in going to and from the bass regulator and implies considerable dexterity on the part of the piper, allied to a remarkably loose wrist, for it must be remembered that while the whole hand is rocking the fingers are moving at great speed on the chanter, particularly in reel-playing. In addition to all this, the piper lifts the chanter from the knee occasionally, as already indicated, and, of course, his right arm is moving out and in to work the bellows while his left arm moves slightly in and out in time with the right arm movements so as to maintain a constant air pressure in the bag under his left arm. As if all this were not enough, he must remember to increase the left arm pressure considerably in playing notes on the higher octave and exert a medium pressure in sounding the hard D. Is it any wonder that the poor uilleann piper may sometimes ponder whether he is actually playing the instrument or is himself being played by it?

It is possible to get single notes on the tenor regulator as well, if these are desired, by a tilting action of the heel of the hand, but it is very difficult to obtain single notes on the baritone regulator unless the right hand is free of the chanter. Two-part chords, using the bass and baritone regulators, are quite simple and are extensively used as shown in Fig. 6.6.

Figure 6.6 Regulator accompaniment using two-part chords

It is important to realise that the so-called full chords available on the regulators are limited to G major, D major and A minor and so are not capable of supplying what might be regarded as full harmony in either G major, D major or their associated minor keys. None of the chords are complete and, even if they were, they could not form the basis for a standard harmonic accompaniment to Irish tunes because of their limited range. This fact in itself should convince pipers that any attempt to provide a full chorded accompaniment throughout a tune is bound to be boring.

The preferred method, and that adopted by the better pipers, is to introduce the regulators during the repeat of the tune or a part of it, as a means of varying the arrangement.

CHAPTER 7

The fiddle

The fiddle and uilleann pipes share between them the distinction of having been vehicles for the expression of Irish traditional music over a period of more than two hundred years. It is true to say that they have shaped the music in a very real sense. Even though the fiddle, unlike the uilleann pipes, has no distinctively Irish features and is, in fact a standard violin, the style of playing adopted by traditional fiddlers has evolved into something distinctive and uniquely suited to Irish music. In particular, the emphasis placed on variation in Irish dance music implies a certain compositional ability in good traditional performers. This composition is done not with a pen and manuscript but on the instrument itself and in this way the instrument leaves its mark on the tunes composed on it, so that many are obviously fiddle tunes while others are equally recognisable as pipe tunes. The distinguishing characteristic may be, for example, a melodic pattern which lies easily under the fingers on one instrument but would be difficult on another or, alternatively, the notes on which decorations occur may give a clue to the origin of the tune. In many cases the range of the tune will indicate that it is basically a fiddle tune rather than a pipe tune.

When discussing the range of the fiddle it must be borne in mind that traditional fiddlers invariably play in the first position, thus giving them a range of just over two octaves, from the note G below middle C to the B above the treble clef. Since they play in the first position, traditional fiddlers are not obliged to grip the instrument firmly between the jaw and shoulder as the classical player would, since his left hand must be able to move up and down the fingerboard to the different positions. This means that there is no absolutely correct way of holding the fiddle in traditional music. Some have it tucked under their chin while others rest it against their chest, shoulder or upper arm. In some cases it is held almost as low as waist level. The neck of the fiddle is usually supported in the palm of the left hand with no serious restriction on the mobility of the fingers as long as only the first position is used. The bow is held lightly between the thumb and fingers of the right hand at or near the nut, though many hold the bow as much as four or six inches away from the end. The method of holding the bow varies enormously, as well as the amount of bow movement employed in playing. Traditional players generally do not utilise the full bow. A very light grip is essential if the fast bowing decorations used in the dance music are to be successfully executed. Some commentators on the traditional scene make almost a fetish of a particular method of holding the bow or the fiddle, forgetting that it is the music that counts and not the stance or the hold. The good traditional fiddler is generally well endowed with common sense and leaves such sterile discussions to those less musical than himself!

Fiddle decorations

The roll

This is the most important decoration used in dance music and consists of the main note and two subsidiary notes, one higher and one lower. The beginning of 'Morrison's Jig' (undecorated) is shown in Fig. 7.1. The decoration on notes E and B is shown in Fig. 7.2(a). The first finger is held down for the main note, the

Figure 7.1 First phrase of 'Morrison's Jig' (undecorated)

Figure 7.2 (a) First-finger roll; (b) second-finger roll; (c) back roll

upper auxiliary note being obtained by a quick flick of the third
finger on the fingerboard and the lower by lifting the first finger
momentarily to let the open string sound a very short note. On
replacing the first finger the main note will sound again. One
might expect the upper auxiliary to be the next highest note above
the main one but in fact it is generally a third above, as in this
example, since the third finger has more freedom to produce the
darting action required. The roll is generally done under a single
bow stroke, though we shall see later that additional emphasis
may be given by a bow change.

A roll on the second finger is shown at Fig. 7.2(b) on the note
F. The upper auxiliary note is still obtained by the third finger and
is in fact the next highest note to the main one.

These rolls are the ones most commonly used. A roll on the third
finger, sometimes called a back roll by traditional fiddlers, is less
common — Fig. 7.2(c). In this roll the little finger is generally
placed in a slightly flat position so that in a roll on the note G
on the D string the upper auxiliary is somewhere between A and
A flat. The actual pitch of auxiliary notes is not important as they
are of such short duration that one might consider them to be
rhythmic rather than melodic devices.

It is, of course, impossible to do a roll like these on an open
string since the lower auxiliary note is not available without
crossing on to the next string, which would be impracticable at
speed. Traditional fiddlers often employ a different form of the
roll in these circumstances and two versions of it on the D string
are shown in Fig. 7.3. Version (a) is the more usual form, using the

(a)   *(b)*

Figure 7.3 Open-string roll

third finger for the G. It is rather more fluid than (b) which uses
the second finger for the F. The fact that the first finger is already
down for the E means that rolling the third finger is much more
effective than rolling the second.

The notation given above for rolls is approximate and reflects the fact that the actual relative length of notes in all fast decorations varies from one performer to another and is an important part of his style. This will be considered in detail later.

Trebling

This is a form of decoration which uses the bow only and consists of a very fast triplet on the note to be decorated. It is shown in Fig. 7.4. Traditional fiddlers tend to do all their trebles with the

Figure 7.4 (a) Treble; (b) Double treble

same bowing and few of them are able to treble with equal facility up and down. It should be pointed out that even though bowing signs are indicated in the figure, the traditional player does not think of it in this way but rather imparts a quick flick to the bow with slight wrist action, and the restoring action of the hand completes the treble. It is all done so quickly and with so little bow movement that it is barely perceptible in performance: one merely hears the marked rhythmic lift that it gives to the music. Trebling can be done on all notes, including those on open strings, making it a very versatile decoration.

A small number of traditional players employ what they call a double treble. It is shown at Fig. 7.4(b) as a group of five separately bowed notes, generally beginning on a down-bow. Since the five notes must be played in approximately the same time as the three notes of the normal treble, it is a very difficult decoration to perform, requiring a double flick of the hand. It is generally restricted to hornpipes or slow reels and even then the adjoining notes should be such as to allow the player to approach it with the bow going in the preferred direction and in the best position for the double-flick. As John Kelly, the noted fiddler, says: 'Doing a double treble is like throwing a jump — you must get your spaces right and your foot down in the proper place to jump.'

Triplets

Various triplets are shown in Fig. 7.5. Those at (a) and (b) would occur either as main notes of a tune or as a decoration of a main note by an upper or lower auxiliary note. These triplets may be

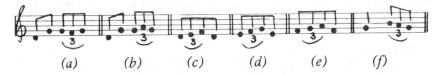

Figure 7.5 Triplets

individually bowed. Separate bowing gives an effect which is not unlike close-fingering on the pipes, and the attack on the notes caused by the bow change gives added 'bite' to the playing. If the first two notes of the above triplets are considerably shortened and the emphasis placed on the last note, the effect is that of a decoration of the last note by the two preceding notes. This is quite common in traditional playing but is not, strictly speaking, a triplet at all.

The triplets shown at Fig. 7.5(c), (d) and (e) generally arise from the filling-in of the interval of a third between two notes. They are shown here on the D string of the fiddle but there are three similar possibilities on the other strings as well. Descending triplets are also quite common. It should be noted that triplets such as that at (f) do not normally occur as decoration, except in slow tunes, since they involve crossing to another string.

The first bar of the reel 'The Broken Pledge' is given in Fig. 7.6 followed by an alternative version showing a common triplet variation on the first beat. The first two notes of the triplet are the same. It is not necessary that its notes be adjacent as in this

Figure 7.6 Possible triplet decoration in 'The Broken Pledge'

95

example, though this is the more usual form. The three notes are separately bowed, though the third may be taken in the same bow as the second.

Cutting

The example at Fig. 7.7(a) shows the beginning of the jig 'Sixpenny Money', illustrating the very effective use of cuts or grace notes to separate the A notes in the first bar. The cutting

(a)   (b)

Figure 7.7 Cuts to separate repeated notes. (a) 'Sixpenny Money';
(b) 'Drowsy Maggie'

notes are here produced by a flick of the third finger on the A string. The note produced, D, has a rhythmic rather than a melodic function and serves to provide an effective attack on the second note without re-bowing. When one is cutting to a note on the third finger there is, of course, no alternative to cutting with the fourth finger.

   A further use of the cut to separate two notes taken in the same bow is shown in the reel 'Drowsy Maggie' at Fig. 7.7(b). The note E at the end of the first bar is separated from the E on the first beat of the second bar by a G cut. Playing the up-beat and the first beat of the bar in the one bow here gives great lift and smoothness to the tune. The new bow taken on the up-beat gives the off-beat emphasis so vital to good dance music, while a slight extra pressure on the main beat gives it the required definition. It is worth pointing out that the whole first bar of this tune can be played without having to move any finger except the third and even that only once to get the note D. The first finger is left down through the bar on both the D and A strings to give the notes E and B. One has only to play this on pipes, flute, whistle, accordion, concertina or any other instrument to realise that it is very much a fiddler's tune!

Cuts are also used to grace an isolated note, the most usual cutting finger being, as before, the third. An example of such cutting is shown in the second half of the jig 'Sixpenny Money'

(a)   (b)

Figure 7.8 Cuts to grace a single note

at Fig. 7.8(a), with a cut from high A to F sharp. This type of note-accentuation is the most common function of the cut and examples of it proliferate in any good traditional fiddler's performance. A cut into a triplet such as that shown at Fig. 7.8(b) is a fairly common device and converts the triplet into a figure approaching a roll. In fact it is sometimes called a short roll, though it seems better to keep the term 'roll' for the figure so described in an earlier section.

Droning

A drone is used to a considerable extent in traditional fiddling. It is produced by drawing the bow across two strings simultaneously while only one of them is being fingered. The drone string is usually the one lower than the fingered string, but in some cases the higher string is used for the drone though this is somewhat more difficult.

A good example of droning is given in the second half of the jig 'The Gander in the Pratie Hole' (Fig. 7.9). Since almost all

Figure 7.9 Droning: second half of 'Gander in the Pratie Hole'

the notes in the first six bars are played on the A string, the D string is almost continously droned. The drone notes are represented here as dotted crotchets but, in practice, the note values of the drone depend on the bowing: each time the melody is bowed a new drone note is initiated. In this way the drone gives considerable rhythmic emphasis to the playing as well as providing its normal function of accompaniment. In this example it will be seen that every time D is in the melody it is reinforced by the D an octave below in the drone, making the melody note ring out in a quite exciting way in performance. Even in situations where continuous droning is not happening, a single note is often emphasised by its lower octave. The lower octave note is the open string, implying that the higher note is obtained by the third finger on the string above it. If the melody note is on the open string, then it may be emphasised in this way by the note an octave above it, which may sometimes act as an upper drone for fingered notes on the lower string. An example of this is shown in Fig. 7.10.

Figure 7.10 Droning: first half of 'Gander in the Pratie Hole'

It may come as something of a surprise to classical musicians to find that the most common drone is the fourth below the melody note, particularly at phrase endings. The first part of the jig 'Gander in the Pratie Hole' shows this occurring at the end of each four-bar phrase, with an A below the final D melody note. An example of droning on the G string also occurs here. A drone a fourth below often occurs in the second half of an E minor tune as shown in Fig. 7.11. Here the note B is held down after it is played as a melody note to provide a drone for the rest of the phrase. A tune in G major often has a B held on the lowest string below a G in the melody tune, or sometimes the B a third above

Figure 7.11 Melody note, B, retained as a continuous drone

may be held instead. Both of these generally occur as single-note accompaniments and not as continuous drones.

The use of double stopping to produce two unison notes is quite common in traditional fiddling. It generally occurs on a long note, usually a dotted crotchet, and is obtained by holding the fourth finger down on the lower string and bowing both it and the upper open string together. The effectiveness of this device is increased if the note on the stopped string is very slightly out of tune with the open string. The piquant sound produced is very characteristic of the fiddle played in traditional style and just cannot be imitated on any other traditional instrument. Since part of the attraction of instrumental playing in the Irish tradition is the freedom that the performer enjoys in interpretation, including the ability to emphasise certain features of the music which are well suited to his instrument, one finds this particular device used frequently by good traditional fiddlers. The long A note in the first bar of the reel in Fig. 7.12 — 'The Repeal of the Union' — is often doubled in this way.

Figure 7.12 Unison double stopping in 'The Repeal of the Union'

Another interesting variation may occur in this tune. Instead of the usual decoration on the D crotchet in the first bar of the tune, the D on the fourth finger on the G string may be used as the middle note of a triplet decoration, the two outer notes of the triplet being the open-string D. The difference in quality between the open and stopped strings, combined with the crossing of the strings to produce the notes, gives just enough change in character to the sound to make it an acceptable variation. One sometimes finds fiddlers using the stopped D as a kind of bridge in going to the open D.

Sliding

Changing the pitch of a note by sliding the finger along the string is not difficult for a fiddler and in certain circumstances it is an accepted traditional method of variation. The slide is always upwards and generally consists of a semitone change in pitch or less. It most commonly occurs on the note F natural at the top of the treble clef and is obtained by moving the first finger on the top string from just above the E position up to the F. To allow the slide to be fully effective, the note slid to must be a long accented note. An example of this on the note B on the A string is shown in Fig. 7.13. The slide might occur by way of variation on the B, as an alternative to the roll which would normally be there. Why

Figure 7.13 Slide on long note, B, as an alternative to the roll or cut shown

does the fiddler slide in this way? It is possible that the slide to F natural may be influenced by the fact that the piper without an extra key on his chanter is obliged to slide to the note and the fiddler playing along with him might imitate such an effective movement. This note is, of course, the flattened seventh in G major and it has already been pointed out that singers also tend to slide to it as it is a note of variable pitch in practice.

Sliding sometimes occurs on the second and third fingers, but it is a little more difficult and the majority of fiddlers do not employ it. An exception to this is the situation where the first finger

1 Maurice Kennedy making uilleann pipe reeds

2 Alf Kennedy making a chanter for a Kennedy set of uilleann pipes

3 Fingering the uilleann pipe chanter

4 Diarmuid Ó Súilleabháin

5 Paddy Keenan

6 Matt Cranitch

has already played its note (B on the A string, for example) and the second finger then rolls on to the note a semitone above (C in this case). This slide is fairly common, particularly in going to the C natural.

Downward sliding is used by a small number of younger fiddlers. It is a regrettable innovation as it is not a natural development from the tradition itself but has its roots in an alien system.

Vibrato

Any general use of vibrato, particularly in dance music, is completely out of place in Irish traditional music and its use is a pretty sure indication that the performer is not a traditional musician. None the less, there are a number of situations in which the very best performers use it even in dance music, and two of them are worth mentioning here since they are really ornamental devices.

In the reel in Fig. 7.14, 'Rakish Paddy', the first C natural is a stressed and important note and generally gets special treatment

Figure 7.14 The reel 'Rakish Paddy': vibrato is usual on the first note

from performers on all instruments. The piper, for example, gives it a very wide vibrato, using the two middle fingers of his right hand to vary the pitch of the note considerably. Some fiddle players use a device which is really half-way between vibrato and a trill, possibly imitating the pipe ornamentation. The fiddler's second finger is placed on the note C natural and the third finger is placed beside it, very near the fingerboard. The hand is then

101

rocked and the resultant sound is not unlike that obtained on the pipes, though the fiddle vibrato is wider.

A form of slow vibrato is sometimes used as a rhythmic variation in dance music of the slower type. Its use is illustrated in the hornpipe 'The Banks of the Ilen' in Fig. 7.15. The crotchet, D,

Fig. 7.15 The hornpipe or reel 'The Banks of the Ilen': slow vibrato could be used on the D note marked in the first bar

requires some form of ornamentation here, normally in a triplet rhythm, as this has already been established on the first beat of the bar and is a common hornpipe decoration. Instead of going to a new note for the middle note of the triplet, the finger is rocked slightly to give a vibrato, as it were, in triplet rhythm. The result is a smooth movement to a triplet middle note microtonally removed from D and back again to D for the last note of the triplet. In practice it is a subtle and effective variation.

Bowing

No analysis of traditional fiddle decorations would be complete without an appreciation of the importance of the bow. The whole character of the music depends on bowing more than on any other single item, and this explains why the various provincial styles of fiddling in Ireland are distinguished more by their bowing variations than by anything else. Some fiddlers would claim to have two instruments, the bow and the fiddle, emphasising the importance they place on bowing. Whatever about this, there is no doubt that fiddle playing has two dimensions, fingering and bowing. In a tradition which employs only the first position in fingering, bowing inevitably assumes prime importance. The fingers do little more than decide which note is to be played and the bow governs just about every other feature associated with it, including initial attack, sound quality, volume, tone variation, time value and even the method of quitting the note.

It has already been pointed out that different bowings will vary the effectiveness of the roll and of the triplet decorations discussed above, while trebling, of course, depends completely on very short fast movements of the bow. In the larger dimension of phrasing in a tune, the bowing decides not only the length of phrase but also the way in which the up-beat may be joined to the main beat or separated from it for special effects. This has already been discussed in the section on cutting, with reference to the reel 'Drowsy Maggie'. Closer examination of the bowing in Fig. 7.16

Figure 7.16 Possible bowing for the reel 'Drowsy Maggie'

shows the notes of the first two bars bowed mostly in pairs, though not in a regular fashion, with the off-beat generally taken under the same bow as the following main beat, the slurs over the notes indicating the bowing. In this example, the notes on the main beats might be regarded as the melody and the off-beat E notes as a kind of drone that the bow keeps touching on the lower string. A slight extra pressure on the off beats makes the melody sing out, while the regular crossing to the lower string gives the figure added rhythmical interest. Since the arm is raised and lowered once in every bow stroke to cross the strings, the figure-of-eight pattern in the bow-arm in the first bar is a further encouragement to the fiddler to maintain the swinging rhythm set up by this method of bowing the tune.

A number of bowing systems, broadly representing the practice of different regions, may be illustrated by considering possible bowings for the first four bars of 'Lord Mac Donald's Reel' in Fig. 7.17. First, it could be separately bowed right up to the last bar, with each note individually bowed until the last four notes are reached: the first three of these would probably be taken under an up-bow and the last one on a down-bow. This results in a reel

Figure 7.17 Possible bowing for 'Lord Mac Donald's Reel'

with crisply enunciated notes and steady, though possibly slightly monotonous, rhythm, unless the performer takes other steps to give it a lift. A second possible method of bowing this tune is indicated by the slurs in the figure. The notes are mostly bowed in groups of three in an irregular fashion so that a feeling of continous smooth flow is maintained with the few separately bowed notes merely providing rhythmic variety. A regular bowing pattern, particularly in regular groups of four, would tend to break up this flow and change the reel into something rather pedestrian and four-square. A third method of bowing would involve taking many more notes under a single bow. In some instances this could be as many as six or eight, though they will usually be taken in an irregular fashion, as explained above, to maintain a smooth fluid rhythm. In this method of playing more attention is generally paid to finger ornamentation and smooth rolls fit easily into the long bowing style.

Tuning

The fiddle is generally tuned to concert pitch, with the four strings being tuned in standard fashion, E A D G. Formerly there was no absolute standard, the D string of the fiddle being tuned to the bottom note of the uilleann piper's chanter, which could have been anything from C down to B flat, depending on the length of the chanter. Fiddlers sometimes use unusual tunings, the most common one being D G D G obtained by letting the two top strings down a tone. This makes the playing of certain tunes much easier and, in particular, the fact that all open strings are either tonic or dominant when playing in the key of G, makes droning and certain other ornamentations more accessible to the performer.

CHAPTER 8

Three musicians

1 Diarmuid Ó Súilleabháin

Diarmuid Ó Súilleabháin comes from the Irish-speaking district of Cúil Aodha in West Cork. The area is rich in traditional music and poetry. Every year in January the School of Poetry meets in Cúil Aodha and invitations are sent to all the poets to assemble and discuss in poetry the theme set out for them. It is an area in which poems and songs are still made about the ordinary events of rural life. It is a part of the general area in which Martin Freeman made his famous collection of songs some fifty years ago.

Traditional singing has been a part of Diarmuid's family for many generations. In his early years, however, even though it was all around him, Diarmuid did not pay too much attention to it. He was attracted to other types of singing and music making and it was some time before he was drawn to the traditional singing which has now become such a major part of his life. None the less, the local singers even then were to have an effect on his singing. Speaking of his father he says:

'Bhal ní deirfinn gur fhoghlaimíos aon cheann uaidh díreach sa tslí sin mar, abair, nuair a bhíos san aos gur cheart domh, beidir, bheith ag foghluim amhráin dá leithéid sin ó dhaoine mar sin is docha gur beag suim a bhí agam ionnta. Ach gidh nar fhoghlaimíos iad d'airíos iad aige agus ansin bhíodar dearmadta agam. Comh fada agus a bhain lem chuimhne bhíodar dearmadta ach ní doigh liom go rabhadar, mar go raibh rian fágtha istigh im aigne in áit éigin agus nuair a thánas trasna na h-amhráin céanna ag daoine eile nó i leabhair nó in aon áit eile go bhféadfainn cuimhniú siar ar conus a dúirt sé siúd iad agus daoine eile a d'áiríos le linn m'óige comh maith gur

chuimhin liom conus mar a dúradar-san iad nó cuid dá ndúradar
go raibh sé éagsúil le mar a áiríos agus go mbfheárr liom an tslí
a raibh sé acu siúd ná an tslí a dh'áiríos é ar tape recorder nó i
leabhar nó pé áit ina bpiocfainn suas amhrán.'

'Well, I wouldn't say I learned any from him directly, in that
way. I suppose when I was at the age when I should have been
learning songs like that from men like him I had little interest
in them. But even though I didn't learn them I heard them and
forgot them again: that is, as far as ordinary memory goes they
were forgotten, but some trace of them was left somewhere in
my mind so that when I hear others singing those songs or if I
came across them in a book or somewhere else I could imagine
how he sang them or how others that I had heard when I was
young, sang them. Sometimes what I might hear would be quite
different from the way they had sung them before and I would
prefer the older way, perhaps, to what someone else might have
on tape or in a book or in any place that I might pick up a
song.'

Apart from his father, Diarmuid was influenced by two well-
known singers of the area, both now deceased — Seán Eoin Ó
Súilleabháin, a relation of his own and a poet as well, and Pádraig
Ó Tuama. Seán Eoin's father, Eoin a' Bháb, and Pádraig Ó Tuama
are regarded by many as probably the best Cúil Aodha singers in
living memory. The author still has vivid memories of the unique
and very personal singing style of Pádraig Ó Tuama. He had the
ability to transform completely a well-known song into something
quite new. One remembers his rendering of 'Cath Chéim an Fhia',
probably the best known song of the area: one's interest was held
in every line as he applied his traditional skill to the reshaping of
the phrases, finding climaxes where one would hardly have expected them and yet being at all times convincing. His use of glottal
stopping and his ability to make pauses for certain effects and still
hold his audience were part of a traditional singing technique that
had been perfected over many years for this same audience.
  It seems to the author that Diarmuid Ó Súilleabháin has many
of Pádraig Ó Tuama's stylistic devices in his singing. Sometimes
these are conscious imitations, modified, of course, to suit

Diarmuid himself, and at other times they are part of the common well of tradition that both singers draw from. Diarmuid remembers a time when Pádraig was encouraging him to sing and showing him how to begin:

'Is cuimhin liom Pádraig Ó Tuama, Domhnach nó rud éigin — is greannmhar an rud mar a chuimhníonn tú ar rudaí mar sin — ach bhíos fein agus lad óg eile thiar, timpeall na Croise áit éigin. Bhí Páidí ann agus is doigh liom go raibh dhá bhata aige an uair sin — ach ar aon chuma thosnaigh sé ag caint leis an mbeirt againn agus dúirt sé: "Is breá a fhéadfadh sibhse amhrán-aíocht dá gcuirfeadh sibh chuige." Dúras nach raibh aon ró-mhaith ionam féin chun amhránaíochta ar chuma éigin.

' "Ní foláir duit tosnú mar seo," dúirt se. "Tá sé an fhuirist. Tosnaigh mar seo anois. 'Cois abhann Ghleann a Chéama' agus nuair a bhíonn tú thíos ansin bíonn tú á rá an-íseal agus ar ndoigh is féidir leat stop agus anál a thógaint," dúirt sé, "agus ní bheidh fhios ag éinne é agus ansin leanúint ort — In Uibh Laoire sea bhím-se — agus mar sin."

'Beidir gur dhúirt sé a lán rudaí eile ach ní chuimhin liom aon rud eile a dúirt sé. D'áiríos é féin a rá an amhráin ina dhiaidh sin agus thógas ceann de'n tslí ina dúirt sé é: d'áiríos é ar théip aige, fiú amháin cúpla version éagsúil de agus d'áiríos, abair, version Béarla aige de'n bhfonn leis na focail "The Cill na Martra Exile" a rá aige ar théip comh maith.'

'I remember Pádraig Ó Tuama one Sunday — it's funny how you remember things like that — with myself and another young lad over there at the Cross somewhere. I think Pádraig was on two sticks at the time. Anyway, he started talking to us, saying, "You could sing well if you really tried." I told him that I wasn't much at singing, anyway.

' "Start off like this," he said. "It's very easy. 'Cois abhann Ghleann a Chéama', and when you're down on that note you're singing very low and you can stop and take a breath and nobody will know. Then you can continue — In Uibh Laoire sea bhím-se, and so on."

'He probably said a lot of other things, but I don't remember now. I heard him singing a song later and I paid particular atten-

tion to the way he sang it. I heard him singing a couple of
versions of it on tape and also the English ballad "The Cill na
Martra Exile" to the same air.'

One of Diarmuid's earliest memories is of the influence of the
poet and local composer and singer, Seán Eoin Ó Súilleabháin,
who used to visit them:

'Bhal, chun dul siar, comh fada siar, is dócha agus a fhéadfainn
dul: an chéad amhrán a bhfuil cuimhne agam ar é a fhoghluim
d'fhoghlamíos é ó Sheán Eoin Ó Súilleabháin. Bhíodh sé siúd
nuair a bhíos an-óg, díreach, abair, ag tosnú ar scoil an uair sin,
bhíodh sé siúd ag scoraíocht sa tigh. Bhí cónaí air, béidir,
míle trasna portaigh is carraigreacha siar uaim agus bhíodh sé
ann oíche sa tseachtain, nó cúpla oíche sa tseachtain agus
bhíodh cur trí chéile — is beag amhráin a bhíodh ann. Bhíos-
sa díreach ag tosnú ar scoil agus bhíodh, tá's agat sa scoil
Ghaeltachta, cúig phunt a bhí ann an uair sin, is dócha go bhfuil
sé tar éis eirí ó shoin, do pháistí a tógtaí le Gaoluinn. Thagadh
cigire uair sa mbliain, nó cúpla uair sa mbliaian chun scrúdú
a dhéanamh ar gach éinne féachaint an raibh Gaoluinn acu
gurbh fhiú cúig phunt í, is docha! Ach an tráth seo, ar aon
chuma, bhí an cigire ag teacht. Bhí Seán Eoin ag scoraíocht an
oíche seo agus béidir go rabhas in áirde ar a ghlúna, ní fheadar,
nó rud éigin agus dúras leis go raibh an cigire ag teacht. Ní
dúirt sé aon ní ach tháinig sé arís an oíche ina dhiaidh sin agus
bhí amhrán déanta aige. Ní chuimhin liom an t-amhrán anois
ná aon ní ach is cuimhim liom gur mhúin sé dhom é. Chuir
sé iachall orm é a fhoghluim — i gcoinne mo thola, béidir, agus
nárbh é an cleas go gcaithfinn é a rá do'n gcigire nuair a
thiocfadh sé ar scoil. Ní rabhas chun faic a rá ach do scéitheadh
orm sa scoil — a rá go raibh a léithéid seo agam agus cuireadh
suas os comhair an chigire mé chun amhráin a rá. Ní chuimhin
liom fonn ná focal ná aon rud eile ach is docha gur lean a
rian im aigne in áit éigin.'

'Well, to go right back, probably as far back as I can remember:
the very first song that I recall learning was from Seán Eoin
Ó Súilleabháin. He used to céilí, or visit, in our house when I
was very young, just starting school. He lived a mile or so

109

across rock and bog, but came visiting one or two nights a week
— it was mostly talk and discussion — not much singing. I was
just starting school and you know how at that time there was
a five pounds grant in Gaeltacht schools — I suppose it's more
now — for children brought up Irish-speaking. The inspector
used to come once or twice a year to inspect the children to
find out, I suppose, if their Irish was worth a fiver! Anyway,
the inspector was due at this time. I think I was sitting on Seán
Eoin's knee when I told him the inspector was coming. He
didn't say anything then but came back the next night with a
song he had just composed. I don't remember anything about
the song itself except that he taught it to me. He made me
learn it — against my will I'm sure — and the idea was that I
should sing it for the inspector when he visited the school.
I wasn't going to say a word about it but someone told on
me and I was put up in front of the inspector to sing the song.
I don't remember the air or the words or anything, but I feel
that it has left its mark somewhere in my mind.'

Diarmuid feels strongly that traditional singing is for him a
personal expression of what both the words and music of the song
mean to him. He believes, in the first instance, in relying on the
tradition that is inbuilt in both himself and in the area, to mould
the song, but does not shield himself from the influence of traditional singers from other areas and acknowledges the influence
of singers like Seán Ac Donncha from Carna, Co. Galway, Seán
de h-Ora from Ballyferriter, Co. Kerry and Nioclas Tóibín from
Ring, Co. Waterford. He first became conscious of a style of his
own when he was part of a group of Cúil Aodha singers meeting in
the house of the late Seán Ó Riada:

'Do mhúin Seán Ó Riada amhrán nach raibh áirithe agam féin
riamh — b'shin "Cúil Duibh-Ré" nó "Cois an Ghaorthaidh".
Is ó Sheán Ó Riada a fuaireas é sin ach bhíodh sé coitianta sa
dúthaigh ach níor áiríos ariamh é go dtí . . . is amhlaidh a
sheinn sé ar phiano do'n gcéad uair dom é. Bhí sé scríofa síos i
leabhar ag an Athair Pádraig Breathnach agus do sheinn sé é
mar a bhí sé se leabhar. Tá cuimhne agam ar seo fós . . . níl's
agam ar cheart dom é a rá nó nar cheart, but anyway. . . .
    'Do mhúin sé an ceol dom, líne ar líne. Ní raibh ann ach

ceithre líne ar aon chuma agus bhí sé fuirist go leor é a
fhoghlaim agus scríobhas síos na focail. Bhíodh cleachtú againn
uair sa tseachtain nó thagaimís le chéile i dtigh an Riadaigh.
Bhí an t-amhrán seo ann agus bhíos ag gabháil de. Nuair a
tháinig an chéad oíche eile bhios ar an gcéad duine istigh nó
bhí cúpla duine eile istigh agus chuir sé céist orm conus a bhí
ag eirí liom leis an amhrán agus dúirt sé liom píosa dhe a rá
dhó ansin. Agus dúirt véarsa dhe agus dhein sé rud a mheasas
a bheith aisteach. Chuaigh sé amach go dtí an cistín agus
ghlaoigh sé isteach ar Ruth agus dúirt leí: "Eist leis seo."
    'Ní raibh's agam céard a bhí ar bun aige. Dúirt sé liom ina
dhiaidh sin gur mhúin sé an ceol díreach mar cheol — go raibh
rud éigin déanta leis agam féin go raibh rudaí breise curtha
isteach, nó rud éigin. Ní raibh 's agam go raibh. Mheasas nach
rabhas ach ag rá an amhráin mar a fuaireas é. Ní fheadar an
amhlaidh a bhíos nó nach rabhas.'

'Seán Ó Riada taught us a song that I had never heard before —
"Cúil Duibh-Ré" or "Cois an Ghaorthaidh". I got it from Seán,
but it had been common in the area long before that, though I
had never heard it until he played it on the piano for me. It was
from Father Pádraig Breathnach's book and Seán played it just
as it was written. I still remember this — I don't know whether
I should tell it or not, but anyway. . . .
    'He taught me the music line by line. There were only four
lines anyway and it was easy enough to learn and I wrote
down the words. The next night I arrived first or else there were
only one or two there and Seán asked me how I was getting on
with the song. He asked me to sing a bit of it and I sang a verse.
Then he did something I thought peculiar. He went out into the
kitchen, called in Ruth and said to her: "Listen to this."
    'I didn't know what he meant. He told me later that he had
taught me the bare notes of the music but that I had made
something else of it, added things of my own. I wasn't aware
that I had, but thought I was singing the song as I had got it.
Goodness knows whether I was or not.'

Diarmuid is primarily a natural unaffected singer with a rich
resonant voice, but he is none the less fully aware that sean-nós

singing is an art that exists on a number of levels — the first being concerned with the normal communication of the meaning of the song to his audience in words. The second might be seen as reflecting his own attitude to the story and being concerned with stylistic devices such as pausing, emphasis, tone of voice, position of climax, etc. Even though such devices inevitably affect the music, their main purpose is not musical but is basically concerned with communication. A third level in sean-nós singing is concerned with the music alone and one feels in listening to Diarmuid Ó Súilleabháin that he pays more than average attention to this aspect of the art. His singing of, for example, 'Marbhna Mhic Fhinghín Duibh' convinces one that he is just as aware of the very impressive musical line as he is of the noble words of the lament. He is continually striving to improve his performance, modelling himself on the older singers of the area, yet going out to meet and compete with other traditional singers, and at the same time learning something from all of them. He is the kind of singer who is admired for his sincerity by other competitors, and he has been All-Ireland champion traditional singer on a number of occasions. How does he himself regard style in singing?

'Bhal, is saghas ruda é a bhfuil sé ana dheacair é a mhíniú. Cuirfidh mé mar seo é — Nuair a áirím é is dóigh liom go n-aithním é, ach ní dóigh liom go bhfuil sé comh fuirist é a chur i bhfocail. Bhal, le h-aon tsaghas amhránaíochta tá binneas gútha, ach arís ní gá gurab shin é is tabhachtaí in amhránaíocht traidisiúnta. Tá stíl iomlán i gcéist. Tá an tslí ina dtugann duine faoi amhrán a rá; ansin an t-amhrán féin. Ní fheadar — abair rud comh simplí leis an áit a dtógann duine anáil: má deintear é sin ag deireadh líne, abair, mar pháiste scoile ag rá píosa filíochta, ag stopadh ag deireadh gach líne, éiríonn sé leamh tar éis tamaill ana-ghairid. Sin ceann amháin des na rudaí — abair, línte a rith isteach ina chéile agus mar sin. Ansin tá slite éagsúla chun béim a chur ar rudaí áirithe ná deintear san amhránaíocht clasaiceach ná a leithéid sin. Ní gá do dhuine a ghlór a ardú chun béim a chur ar rud, béidir gur stop roimis nó stop ina dhiaidh nó an tslí ina ndeirtear é. Ansin, gan dabht, tá na casaidheacha go léir, na saghasanna éagsúla dhíobh — na cinn dúbalta agus mar sin, agus tá, abair, sleamhnú ó nóta

112

amháin isteach sa gceann eile agus béidir nóta a mhaolú nó a ghiorru de réir brí na h-amhránaíochta. Na rudaí seo go léir, i dteannta a chéile. Ní gá go mbéidís go léir in aon amhrán — ach cuid díobh le h-aithint i dteannta a chéile chun aonad amhráin go n-aithním-se, ar aon chuma, gur rud éigin fiúntach atá ann.'

'Well, it's the kind of thing that's very hard to define. Can I put it this way — when I hear it I think I recognise it but I don't think it's easy to put into words. For any kind of singing a good voice is desirable but it's not necessarily the most important thing in traditional singing. The overall style is what matters — the approach to the song and, of course, the song itself. I don't know — take for example a simple thing like breathing. If you take a breath at the end of every line, like a child reciting poetry, it becomes boring after a very short while. That's one thing, for example, running the lines into each other. Then there are various ways of making emphasis that are not used in classical singing or that kind of thing. A person doesn't have to raise his voice to emphasise something — he can pause before it or after it or say it in a certain way. Then, of course, there are the various ornamentations, double ornaments and so on. One can slide from one note to another and perhaps flatten a note somewhat or even shorten (sharpen?) it according to the meaning of the song. All these sort of things together are style: they don't all have to be in one song but some of them should be evident together to make a unit that I would recognise as something worthwhile.'

The examples of Diarmuid's singing noted here reveal many other points of style. The notes to the songs detail the various stylistic aspects of his singing.

The songs

'Cúil Duibh-Ré'   This song is also known as 'Cois a' Ghaorthaidh' and is one of the best known songs of the west Cork Gaeltacht area. The poet compares the wildness and barrenness of the area to the west, where the river Lee is rough and untamed, with the area beside him at the Gaortha. Here all is peaceful and prosperous and the people are hard-working.

Diarmuid learned it from Seán Ó Riada who, as was pointed out earlier, was surprised at Diarmuid's unconscious re-creation of the song. His style can best be studied by referring to the musical notation in Fig. 8.1. It is written without bar-lines, though the

Figure 8.1 'Cúil Duibh-Ré'

phrases are clearly between the breathing signs (marked with a V). The main beats are, as always in sean-nós singing, decided by the text. Thus the main beats of the first line are on 'scias-, Laoi, eadar, -niar', and these correspond with the main beats in the second line '— coimheas-, liag-, ceo, niamh'. It can be seen that in the music all such words are associated with relatively long and undecorated notes, so that the main beat in each case is enunciated clearly and unambiguously in the song. The normal vowel assonance ensures a very well defined melodic pattern. The initial consonant in each case, or even sometimes the vowel, is subject to quite a firm attack and is not softened in the way that is normal in English singing. It is usually quitted gently with a decoration, so that the ear is led smoothly to the next main beat. In many ways the effect can be compared with that of good off-beat lift in a dance tune. Both, in their different ways, give life and movement to the music. Small changes in pitch on some notes are indicated by a rising arrow above the note, while the vertical arrow at the end of line 5 represents a glottal stop.

Five sections of the song, marked A, B, C, D and E respectively, have been chosen to examine possible variations in Diarmuid's singing. The opening phrase at A is changed to a rather more decorated version shown at A1 for most of the other verses. Similarly B1, a somewhat more ornamented version of B, is used in later verses. C is unchanged throughout, while D is changed slightly as shown in D1, to match the text in later verses. One feels that section E, following the glottal stop, is given special emphasis. It has already an important position musically, being the climax of the carry-over phrase from the third line and one is aware of the singer's determination to highlight the phrase at each new appearance, either by increasing the degree of ornamentation or by removing it completely to leave only the main notes. This last is particularly effective.

'An Chúil Duibh-Ré'

Nach dúch sciasmhar an Laoi seo gabháil eadaraibh aniar,
Na tuilte coimheascar de bhárr liagreach gan ceó glan niamh.
Níl innseacha lena taoibh ann ná pór breá ar fhéar
Ach barra fraoigh ar charraig aoird ann is nach trua bhur scéal.

Cois a' Ghaorthaidh is breátha in Eirinn 'sis áilne ar abhainn:
Mil is céir bheach, tortha ar ghéaga agus úll ar chrann.
Chloisfeadh éinne cantain éan ann a bheadh míle ón mball:
Cnó buí is caora ar bharraibh géaga a' fás go Samhain.

Nuair a ghabhann sí Drom na Carra soir is ón dteorainn
                                                    riabhaigh
Is taithneamhach gach caise aici le ceó glan niamh.
Bíonn barra glas ar mhaiseannaibh agus pór breá ar fhéar,
Agus cantain suilt i mbarra coille ag ceol na n-éan.

'Sar Tuin soir bíonn ceolta ann agus Aifreann Dé
Fearaibh óga nárbh eol dóibh 'dtigh a taibhirne 'ghlaoch.
Ní le mórtas den tsórt san a bheirid leo an sway,
Ach ag déanamh bóithre le fórsa tríd an gCúil Duibh-Ré.

'An Chúil Duibh-Ré' — 'The Dark Nook'

What a sad and doleful river Lee you have in the west
With floods fighting over the stones and no clean shining mist —
No meadows by its banks nor fine grass growing,
Only heather crop on high rocks. What a pity!

Here beside the Gaortha, the finest river in Ireland
There's honey and beeswax, fruit on the branches and apples
                                                    on the trees:
Anyone could hear a mile off the singing of birds,
And yellow nuts and berries grow on bushes till November.

When it flows past Cara's hill and beyond the grey borders
Every stream is beautiful with that clean shining mist:
There are green crops in the fields and fine grass too,
And the woodtops are filled with joyous bird-song.

In Toon in the east Mass is said and there's music,
And young men who don't call drinks at the bar:
It's not with that sort of boasting that they hold sway,
But by forcing roads with their strength through the Cúil
                                                    Duibh-Ré.

'Carraig Aonair' This is a father's lament for his three sons
drowned near Fastnet Rock, Co. Cork. The fourth man mentioned
is his son-in-law. The father was Conchuir Ó Laoire and the three
sons were Finín, Cormac and Dónal, though I have heard another
version giving the name Tomás instead of Finín.
    The music is a simple two-line melody sung twice for each verse.

It could be boring, but is certainly not so, due mainly to the fine poetry of the text and to the imaginative singing of Diarmuid Ó Súilleabháin.

The notation of the first verse is given in Fig. 8.2. There are only minor changes in succeeding verses — almost all governed by

Figure 8.2 'Carraig Aonair'

textual considerations. One of them in particular is worth special notice, as it clearly shows how a good traditional singer's ornamentation is governed by the words and is restricted by the necessity to communicate the meaning of the song clearly. The opening up-beat of the music in the first verse is on a single syllable 'o', and is also on a single syllable 'ag' half-way through the verse. The singer has therefore decorated it as shown at A and B, since it is a relatively long note and intelligibility is not affected. However, in later verses, when there are two syllables in this position the figure is changed to the more simple shape shown at A5 and B5.

Here the decoration becomes two undecorated notes for 'is in-' at the beginning of the verse and 'Ach ní-' in the middle of the verse. In the fourth verse there are three syllables in this position for 'thugadh a' and the change in the melody is indicated at B4.

The breathing points marked at the end of the second line and in the middle of the last line of the music are sometimes transformed into glottal stops in later verses of the song or, alternatively, as in the sixth verse, the pause becomes a glottal stop at the end of the next word (in this case 'agus') which is fully decorated. Then the last three words of the verse, 'chaoinfinn iad siúd' (I would lament them), coming after the abrupt stop and sung without any decoration at all, are highly dramatic.

The notes marked with an arrow are approached by a slide from below. It is normally about a semitone, but in some verses approaches a full tone. Even though a slide does not occur in the first verse on the E flat in the fourth line, it is approached from below in subsequent verses.

'Carraig Aonair'

O Luan dubh an áir, tháinig suaimhneas ró-bhreá
Is do ghluaiseadar uaimse leath-uairín roimh lá,
Ag iascaireacht i mbád i gcontúirt a mbás:
Go mbeidh iarsma na bliana úd ina ndiaidh go bhfaighfead bás.

Sé Dónal mo mhaoin, an té b'óige dem chloinn
Agus coicíos ón lá sin a tháinig sé i dtír,
Gan tapa gan bhrí gan anam ná chroí
Ach a ghéaga bhoga gheala is iad leata ar a dtuinn.

Sé Cormac mo stór, sé Rí na bhfear n-óg
A bhí modhuil maiseach múinte géar-chumtha go leor:
Do scríobh sé ar a gcóir leis an mbúcla bhí na bhróig
Gurab i Carraig Aonair a chéile go deo.

Tá duine eile dem chloinn nár thráchtas air puinn —
Finín mo chomhgarach ceann cothuithe an tí,
Thugadh a' fia leis on gcoill is an bradán ón linn
Fideóga dubha an tsléibhe is gan bhréig an chearc fraoigh.

Is iníon ó mo chroí ná goil-se 'sná caoidh,
Mar gheoidh tú togha nuachair dhéanfaidh rómhar duit is crích:
Ach ní bhfaigheadsa mo mhaoin ná mo thriúr d'fhearaibh grinn,
Ná mo cheathrar bhreá gléghil de lúbairibh groí.

Sí an Nollaig seo chughainn an Nollaig gan fonn
Ar mo cheathrar bhreá bhruinn-gheal 'tá fé shruthaibh na
                                                    dtonn.
Dá bhfaighinn-se mo thriúir ó go doimhin ins an úir
Is ró-bhreá do shínfinn agus chaoinfinn iad siud.

Is a chlann ó mo chroí nó an cuimhin libh mar a bhí
Bhur n-áthairín bocht féinig ag géar-ghol is ag caoi:
Na chuaille throm chríon i gcúl-fuar a' tí,
Is bhur lúth-chairde féinig ag casadh mar a bhí.

Nuair a théimse ar a gclaí: nuair a fhéachaim uaim síos:
Nuair a chím Carraig Aonair sea phléascann mo chroí;
Is arais liom arís go mullach mo thí,
Os is í Carraig Aonair is céile dhom chloinn.

'Carraig Aonair' —'The Lone Rock' (Fastnet)

On that black Monday of destruction a too-fine stillness came
And away they went from me, half an hour before the dawn,
Fishing in a small boat — in danger of death —
That year's terrible memory will be mine till I die.

Dónal was my pet, the youngest of the clan
And a fortnight from that morning he came to the shore —
Without vigour or strength, without heart or soul,
His soft white limbs frozen and bleached by the waves.

My Cormac was king of all the young men —
Modest and mannered, handsome, well-made:
He wrote on the rudder with the buckle of his shoe
That lone Fastnet rock was his spouse for all time.

There's one more of my clan I've not mentioned yet —
Finín my eldest, the head of the house:
He'd bring deer from the wood and salmon from the pool,
Black plover from the hill and grouse, too, of course.

119

Dear daughter mine don't mourn and cry
For you'll find another husband that will labour for you:
But where can I find the wealth that has gone —
Four big strong men and three fine sons.

Next Christmas is a Christmas that I don't relish
With those four bright children beneath the swirling sea:
If I had my three darlings deep in their graves,
I'd have laid them out nicely and keened them full well.

Dear family of my heart do you remember then
Your own poor father weeping and mourning:
Old and useless in a cold corner of the house
And your dearest friends all complaining.

When I go on the ditch and look away down
And see Fastnet Rock, my heart fairly breaks.
I come back again to the top of my house
For lone Fastnet Rock is my family's spouse.

Commercial recordings

Diarmuid has not, at the time of writing, recorded a solo album, but his singing may be heard on the Ceoltóirí Laighean albums (*An Bothar Cam (The Crooked Road)* — Gael-Linn CEF 035; *The Star of Munster* — Gael-Linn CEF 047).

2 Paddy Keenan

Paddy Keenan is a young piper. He is the third generation of Keenan pipers and is unquestionably the finest of them. His father, John, himself a fine piper, and his brothers who play a little, all acknowledge Paddy as the master.

He began to play the pipes at twelve years of age, having played the tin whistle for some years before that, as well as experimenting with other instruments. His father made him a bag, bellows and chanter and gave it to him one morning, saying: 'If you can play a tune when I come back tonight, I'll see what I can do about getting you the full set of pipes.' Paddy could play part of the reel 'Rakish Paddy' on the chanter that evening and his piping career started forthwith, under his father's tuition.

John Keenan, senior, was a hard taskmaster as John Connors, their neighbour and a fine musician himself, testifies:

'By God, I'm telling you Paddy learned the hard way. He got Paddy up in this room in the house and for three solid hours that chap had to get on there and if he made a mistake at all — a slap on the lug. It was beaten into him and that's how he has it today. It was beaten into him. If he made a mistake: "Quit!" A slap across the face. "Quit! You're not to make a mistake there. I'll put out this light: you'll get no light for an hour. I'll go down to the kitchen and if I hear a mistake I'll come up and I'll do this with you and I'll do that with you." He had to learn it the hard way.'

Paddy himself is aware that his own piping is something special but he is very modest about it. He is aware that his style stems from that of the famous piper Johnny Doran and he has consciously fashioned his piping on the Doran style, via his father, and with the assistance of old recordings made by the Irish Folklore Commission. He is somewhat reticent about discussing himself and his piping method lest anyone should feel that he is, as he says himself, 'big-headed'.

'Most of the pipers today are Rowsome's pupils — they all seem to have the same style — it's open style — a nice style, but nothing special about it. I prefer a mixture of a lot, but flowing in the Johnny Doran way. There was a sort of a wildness in his playing. . . . There's not very many really good pipers around. . . . When you look back on the people who are dead, Touhy, Doran, Cash, you know you wouldn't have much time for listening to the pipers of today. Most of them are so big-headed about their styles, too. They won't stop and listen for a while and find out what it's all about.'

The author has never before encountered such a complete piper. There seems to be no aspect of uilleann piping in which he is not expert. His chanter playing has all the fluid movement that one associates with the travelling pipers of a previous generation. Close and open fingering come equally easily to him and the double or treble rolling so typical of Johnny Doran is possibly the most significant and characteristic aspect of his chanter playing.

Paddy himself is responsible for a number of piping innovations. Possibly the most controversial among pipers is his introduction of a very fast treble or double treble on the back D note of the chanter, not unlike the bowed treble that the fiddler gets on the open string. The reaction of many pipers to this is that it is just not traditional piping. While this is certainly true, it nevertheless remains a fact that the piper was unable to perform any very convincing decoration on the back D note before the introduction of this Keenan treble. It may be argued against its use that the basis of good piping decoration is variety in the successive notes used in decorations, as witness the traditional rolls, cutting and cranning used by all pipers. None the less, the very same arguments could be used against trebling on the fiddle. It seems to the author that Keenan's inventiveness here has filled a gap in piping technique and has created a piping decoration which is already taking its place in the tradition.

Paddy Keenan's use of the bottom hole on the chanter is again an illustration of his inventive approach to piping. The majority of pipers do not move the little finger independently but generally move it and the third finger together to move from low D to E. The author has heard a small number of pipers, notably Seamus Ennis, use the little finger for E flat in jumping up to a higher note on the chanter, particularly in air-playing, but none of them uses it in the chromatic movement from E to E flat and back to E that Paddy Keenan employs in a few tunes. Purists, of course, would criticise the introduction of the chromaticism into diatonic tunes but Paddy Keenan uses it very tastefully and effectively in a small number of tunes, at least one of which was composed by himself.

His accompaniment on the regulators is certainly the most enterprising and at the same time possibly the most subtle that the author has heard. One is struck by the change in his style of regulator playing over a number of years. Old tapes show that he formerly played the normal continuous vamping style employed by most pipers. The change to a more subtle and artistic method was a conscious one, based on a study of old recordings of Johnny Doran:

'When I was younger I used to play double beat through a tune — it was all bump-bump-bump with the tune itself, and it wasn't until I heard Doran's playing, you know, that I got the regulatoring I have today — in between hold-on, trebling, doubling — it's a mixture of the lot. It's a lot nicer, too.'

As far as Paddy Keenan is concerned one cannot be a piper if one does not play the regulators, and his own mastery of them is complete. Sometimes he uses the heel of the hand, while at other times he strikes the top regulator with his wrist, well above the joint. There is not really any obvious repetitive pattern in his playing such as one meets in the playing of most other pipers: he is just as likely to hold a long single note as play a series of vamping chords or pick out a counter-melody on the regulators with his right hand, and his accompaniment can change fundamentally when the tune is repeated.

He arranges the top two regulators to face each other so that they are close together for chord playing and he tunes the bass regulators away from them, towards his body, thus leaving the centre regulator easily accessible for single notes. This would be very difficult with the standard regulator layout. The fact that the bass regulator is turned towards him makes it easily available for the playing of single notes. Its position also brings it near the chanter and makes possible another Keenan innovation, the playing of bass notes, particularly B and C, with the thumb, while both hands still play the chanter.

Paddy has a very keen ear and this has a considerable influence on his regulator playing as it often decides which note he plays:

'If I was playing for a while in a warm place and the pipes were going out of tune I might be off — say the A in the tenor — so I'd pick out single keys, the ones that are in tune. . . . I've sort of got used to it, but mostly I like to get a chord. Even on a sharp tap I like to get the full chord there.'

He is certainly the most fastidious tuner of pipes that the author has encountered. In between tunes he continues to adjust reeds and drones and even slits rushes to insert in the regulators to compensate for pitch changes caused by the heat of the room. All this is not the kind of affectation practised by some older pipers but is done quickly and efficiently. He knows what he wants and gets it without undue fuss. Even pieces of sticking plaster are taken out of his pipe-box to half-cover the holes of notes which have risen in pitch, and he is not averse to sandpapering a reed between performances. The overall result is, of course, music which is in tune at all times. Unfortunately this is not so common as it should be among other pipers.

He is a fine reed-maker and has made reeds for at least one pipe maker as well as keeping his own pipes well fitted with them. His reed-making started before he began to play the pipes, and he learned this skill from his father. His first reeds were made from elder, as there was an elder tree growing beside the house. He has memories of himself and his father playing pipes until five o'clock in the morning and being thankful for the tone of the elder reeds, which was quieter than cane and so more acceptable to neighbours, not to mention one's own family, at that time of day!

Paddy's pipes were made by Denis Crowley of Cork, who died some years ago, and the chanter by the lately deceased Leo Rowsome of Dublin. Paddy himself has replaced both bag and bellows with ones of Keenan manufacture.

His attitude to reed-making is unusual. The measurement of the reed-staple and the cane and bridle details are normally carefully guarded secrets, but while he admits to having got his reed-making skill from his father and some measurements from Matt Kiernan, who makes chanters, he does not believe in slavishly following measurements. His good ear enables him to adjust the finished product to correct tuning and allows for considerable tolerance in the initial staple and cane measurements:

> 'Making reeds and that, you've got to have a good ear. I mean, there's no sense in making a reed, calling yourself a reed-maker, if you can't tune them. It's a good thing to make your own reeds anyway.'

The various points of Paddy Keenan's technique enumerated above, and the details of his approach to piping, still leave one far short of a proper appreciation of his style. Certainly a knowledge of the sum total of his technical achievements does not prepare one for the excitement of his playing. His fluid rolling style of piping is further heightened by his sure instinct for the right place to decorate the melody or even to interrupt its flow by a staccato passage of exceptional brilliance. All the time one feels a kind of controlled wildness in the playing, reminiscent of the famous travelling piper Johnny Doran. The same approach to performance is evident — a willingness to risk everything for success, all the time reaching out for the difficult but rewarding turn or variation rather than taking the easy way around a musical problem. One gets the impression of a performance which is not, as it were, pre-programmed, but is allowed to find its own way into situations which call for improvisation of a high order to bring one back to comparative safety.

'There's a lot of things I do on a chanter, say, that other pipers don't do. I don't really think a lot about it. I like to be able to do it and all that but you get so used to doing it, you know. I've been doing it for years now, playing the same way: it's improving all the time. It's like I play a tune once and play it again, it's different — you'd never hardly play it the one way: well I don't think I do, anyway. I just sit and play and let it come. I don't really think about how I'm going to play it or what I'm going to play or what I'm going to do, or maybe a split second before I do it I'll think about it and shove it in.

'You can destroy a tune by putting too much of something into it, like too much rolling, too much tight fingering or something like that. You've got to have the right place to put it and know when you're putting it there and he [Johnny Doran] had it, you know. . . .'

A study of the music noted here should convince one that Paddy Keenan also has this gift.

The tunes

'Paddy Keenan's Jig' This was composed by Paddy himself and is a good example of a newly-composed tune which sits very comfortably among its older companions. The chanter work is precise and unhurried throughout and the variations are subtle and unforced. The most notable variation is in the regulator work.

The decoration marked C in the first bar of the tune is a closed roll played tightly. Thus the lower note of the roll is absent and this results in the decoration shown. In later repetitions of the tune a slide from the note below is substituted for this and makes

125

Figure 8.3 'Paddy Keenan's Jig'

a very effective variation. The decoration at D is similarly treated. The roll at E is played tightly every time. The melody at G is changed on all subsequent appearances and the bottom D shown here is replaced by a repeated B note. The closed roll at H is

Figure 8.3a 'Paddy Keenan's Jig' (continued)

sometimes replaced by a single cut. The decoration marked J
consists of a slide from F sharp to G. This is later changed to a roll
on the G or else the F sharp is lengthened to become a quaver and
the subsequent crotchet on G is shortened to become a quaver,
as shown on the last appearance of the phrase. The decoration at
K is changed subsequently, so that instead of the cut before the
F sharp it is approached by a slide from the E note in the previous
bar, as shown in B4.

The regulators are not sounded during the first sixteen bars of the tune, but are used in all the subsequent sections except B4. Every single section is given its own different accompaniment, whether it be the off-beat opening of B2, followed by snappy chords on the tenor and baritone regulators, or the long held-notes on the bass regulator, as illustrated in A4. The high B held on the tenor regulator at the beginning of A5 is particularly effective. In the absence of regulators in B4 the piper takes the opportunity to show us some very nice sliding on the notes marked with an X.

I have heard other recordings of this tune, played by Paddy, and have noted quite different regulator accompaniment in each case.

'The Steampacket' This reel, also widely known as 'The Mountain Lark', is a very popular piper's tune. It is basically simple, indeed the core of the first half is a two-bar phrase and the same could be said of the second half as it is based on a similar two-bar melody. The piper's problem is to maintain the listener's interest throughout the many repetitions of such basically simple material. Paddy Keenan does this admirably.

He begins in a relaxed fashion with a nice open roll in the first bar (marked C). Later in the tune this becomes a closed roll. The figure in the second half of the first bar and the similar melody at D are changed frequently throughout the tune to the cran decoration shown at F. A comparison of the opening notes of the first bar with the corresponding sections later in the tune will show that Paddy keeps varying this bar so that no two successive openings are the same. The cran at E and the similar one at G are later changed to a simple quaver figure, as in A3, or to a repeated cran on the note D, as in the last bar of A3. The triplet indicated at H is the 'rubbed' triplet on the back D, already referred to.

The first eight bars are played without regulators, which are then introduced gradually in the second half without, at first, any attempts at rhythmic lift. In A2, B2, A3 and B3 there is considerable crotchet movement of the regulators and at the brisk speed of the tune this gives it great 'life'. One is aware here of the piper's dexterity in maintaining such movement with his wrist while continuing to play the chanter in a 'tight' fashion.

Figure 8.4 Reel: 'The Steampacket'

Commercial recordings

Paddy is the only one of the three musicians mentioned here who has made a solo album. It contains different versions of both of the above tunes, as well as many other fine examples of his piping (*Paddy Keenan* — Gael-linn CEF 045). He may also be heard on the Bothy Band albums (*The Bothy Band* — Mulligan LUN 002; *Old Hag You have Killed Me* — Polydor 2383 417; *Out of the Wind and into the Sun* — Polydor 2383 456).

3 Matt Cranitch

Matt is from Cork and belongs to a very well known musical family. Most of the music was on his father's side of the house though his mother played the piano and sang. His paternal grandfather played the melodeon and did some step-dancing. His uncles and aunts, though not singers, would all sing at a wedding.

His first fiddle teacher was his father, who plays traditional fiddle and accordion and can sing too:

> 'I got my first fiddle as a Christmas present when I was five or six years old and it was decided that my father would give me lessons on Saturday mornings. These continued for some time, but took the form of performances by him for the full half-hour or hour or whatever it was, after telling me that this was how it should be done. My mother then decided that a different method should be tried and they set about getting lessons for me in the School of Music in Cork.'

This decision meant in fact that his music subsequently developed along two quite separate and non-interacting lines: classical and traditional. How had it happened that he became a traditional musician?

> 'Well, that was what was played at home. I think the first traditional tune I learned at home was "Eibhlín a Rúin". Certainly my father's background was all traditional. As we grew up he used to play the accordion with Eilís, Bríd, Peadar and myself on fiddles and whistles or flute. We had a family band and played at concerts and Fleadhanna Ceoil — that's how the interest in traditional music grew: This was going on alongside

the School of Music teaching and certainly there was no cross-fertilisation or interference.'

He found it hard to pinpoint the influence of particular fiddlers on his own style, feeling that he tended to absorb what he heard and thought good, regardless of who played it:

'I am influenced by nearly all traditional players, good and bad: the terms good and bad are, of course, very subjective and you can often learn a lot from a player who is not considered to be in the first category. Nowadays one hears so many recordings of players with a wide variety of styles: we are no longer dependent on the local musician and it is hard to be specific about influences on one's playing.

'Styles now tend to be individual or personal, rather than regional as they were in the past. You hear so much that your own way of playing may be a mixture — not any one style. I always liked listening to the late Denis Murphy from Gneev-guilla, Co. Kerry. He didn't rely too much on what I'd call externals, like obvious trebles or rolls: he used the bow subtly to give an off-beat rhythm. He didn't use the left hand too much for ornamentation, but his right hand was marvellous: when I say marvellous, I don't mean it from the point of view of tone, quality or anything like that — just the great spirit, life and rhythm he gave to the music. When playing a long note in a dance tune he could give the impression of alternately leaning heavily and lightly on the bow for rhythmic effect, without in any way disturbing the flow of the music.'

Matt himself is a meticulous player; every note must be in its right place in time and pitch and the tone must be just as he wants it. He rarely makes a mistake and his approach is not unlike that of piper Paddy Keenan. Both have the top-class instrumentalist's highly self-critical attitude. Nevertheless, Matt always emphasises the importance of listening more for what the musician is playing rather than concentrating on the non-essentials of the process.

'Even if the notes are a bit scratchy, you shouldn't listen to the scratches in case you miss the music! . . .

'I know what a good traditional fiddler is and I can recognise a good one when I hear him, but I find it difficult to define. Dance music must have the vitality and spirit that will make people want to dance. Good tone, in the accepted sense of the word, is not important nor is it necessary to have a good quality fiddle. What makes a good fiddle player is not too different, in many ways, from what makes a good piper: there must be rhythm and verve in the playing, with just the right amount and mixture of ornamentation — of course in fiddling this includes bowing technique. Having said that, you have to realise that a good fiddler is so much more than the sum total of all the techniques and ornamentations we have mentioned. You're in danger of equating all these things with traditional fiddling. Yet, you can teach someone all the tricks and still not have a traditional fiddler.'

Not too many musicians play slow airs well. There is a marked reluctance even to attempt them, mainly due, one feels, to the player's lack of confidence in his tone production. For a long time now Matt Cranitch has been an outstanding slow-air player. He thinks deeply about his method of playing and is committed to a style which, while vibrant, avoids the pitfall of over-sentimentality, remaining faithful to the original song yet creating something new!

'Some notes are more easily emphasised and lie in a better position for ornamentation than others and so there will probably be a small change in the melody compared with the way it is sung. The singer's ornamentation might be imitated on the fiddle, but one wouldn't follow it exactly. You would give the tune what I call fiddle ornamentation, emphasising and decorating different notes. You wouldn't, for example, put a roll on an open string but you could certainly imitate the singer's glottal stop on the fiddle and it does in fact sound good.
    'Some people say you should use vibrato — others say it is wrong to do so. I think myself that the heavy wide vibrato, as taught in music schools, is not correct and I would say that no vibrato at all is preferable. However, if you listen carefully to a singer you will hear a slow, narrower and more relaxed type of vibrato, if you can call it that. This is what I aim for.
    'In playing a slow air you start out taking the tune as it is and using a very light type of vibrato to emphasise some part of

the tune as you want to, or as a singer might do. Certainly I would consider vibrato merely as an element of technique rather than a fundamental part of slow-air playing. When I play slow airs some notes may not have any vibrato at all — others a little, depending on what I want to do at the time. It's not unlike early Baroque fiddle playing, where vibrato was only used to emphasise or heighten some notes. It's a pity that vibrato is taught nowadays as a basic and continuous element of violin playing, rather than for occasional emphasis.'

The slow air noted here, 'Maidin Ró-mhoch' ('Early one morning'), is one that Matt got from the well known singer and player, Seán de h-Ora, who lives in the Irish-speaking area near Ballyferriter in Co. Kerry.

'I had heard Seán singing the song once or twice but had never come across it anywhere else. I asked him if I might tape it and I've played it a few times since. I don't think it's often heard, maybe because of its wide range — from A down on the G string up to G or A on the E string, a full two octaves. This puts it out of the range of many singers and also of pipes, whistle and flute.

'I don't know where Seán got the song. He said something at the time about having it for ever and always and that was it. It's an interesting tune, and if he does know where it came from, I'd like to find out. I think he had only two verses of it at first and the late Seán Ó Riada wrote a third for him. I saw this third verse, in Seán Ó Riada's handwriting, displayed in a place of honour in Seán's house.'

The tunes

'Jenny's Welcome to Charlie' This four-part reel, something of a showpiece among fiddlers, is here given a performance of integrity and spirit. The first section, with its lively triplets (two of them are nice examples of trebling), is repeated without variation. While in general the rolls throughout this tune are indicated by the sign placed over them, the one in bar 6 is written out in full as all its notes are given equal weight, unlike the normal roll illustrated in the chapter on the fiddle. The long F natural in the

Figure 8.5 'Jenny's Welcome to Charlie'

first bar of section B1 is replaced very effectively in the repeat by a four-quaver figure starting on E. Half-way through the section the syncopated roll on the F natural is an arresting decoration.

There are some interesting differences between sections C1 and C2. The last bar of C1 is descending towards the low D that is the first note of C2, and the jump right up to the high A is in striking contrast to the small movement from high E at the beginning of the previous section. The extra triplets in bars 3 and 4 of C2 give a further rhythmic variation.

Bowed triplets were discussed in the chapter on the fiddle and there are examples indicated in sections D1 and D2, bowing being shown in each case. Droning on the D string occurs in bars 3 and 5 of section D2 and the roll combined with the drone is, in both cases, quite exciting. The texture of the music is thickened and a further dimension added, particularly in bar 3 when the drone comes after the complete stop indicated by the quaver rest.

'Maidin Ró-mhoch'   This is the air of the song mentioned above, that Matt got from the singing of Kerryman Seán de h-Ora. Matt has produced an impressive slow air, faithful to Seán's original song, yet subtly shaped and moulded to suit the fiddle. I have heard Matt introduce droning and even a small amount of what is almost a counter-melody on some other airs, but in this one he prefers to keep the treatment of the air quite simple. This suits the mood and poignancy of the very beautiful music. The decorations noted here have grown from Seán de h-Ora's vocal ornamentation, though they are now clearly based on fiddle techniques.

'Maidin Ró-mhoch'

Eistigh seal liom go neósfad scéal díbh
Ar mo chúrsaí féinig nár dhein mo leas:
Do thugas-sa tréimhse ar bhárr na maolchnoc
I dtúis mo shaoil agus mé im fhear chaol dheas.
Do bhíodh na héisc sa tsróill ag léimrigh
Agus ceol na n-éan go binn lem' ais,
Agus mise ag pléireacht le mná ná raibh aosta,
Is dar ndóigh mé 'glaoch ortha sa tigh tabhairne isteach.

Figure 8.6 '*Maidin Ró-mhoch*'

Maidin ró-mhoch do ghabhas an cóngar
Ag déanamh eolais chun luí na mbreac,
Sea dhearcas smólach de chailín gleoite
Ag bailiú cnó buí i gcúl lem' ais.
An croí im bhrollach do phreab ar neomat,
Sé dúirt ba chóir dom bheith páirteach
Sé dúirt sí, a stróinse, tá'n tú pósta
Nó cad is dóigh leat, níl tnú agam leat.

A chailín óig dhíl, sa rí-bhean ró-dheas
Eist lem' scéal-sa is suigh lem' ais,
Mar nílim pósta ná fós im stróinse,
Ach is buachaill óg mé gan mhaoin gan mheas.
Ach gaibh-se im chóngar a phlúir na n-óigbhean,

A réilteáin bhéal-tais bí grámhar seal:
Is bead-sa ag pógadh mo mhíle stóirín
Is ag seimint ceoil duit go dtí lá na gceart.

'Early One Morning'

Listen till I tell you my story
Of what happened to me — and not for my good.
I spent a while on the bare hill-tops
When I was a young and healthy lad.
The fish in the river were all a-leaping
And the song of the birds was sweet nearby
And I was sporting with fine young maidens
Inviting them in to the tavern with me.

One morning early I took a short-cut
Trying to find where the trout did lie
When I saw a fine young shapely damsel
Gathering ripe nuts in a grove nearby.
My heart gave a leap at that very moment
Telling me I should give her love,
But she said, 'Stranger, you are married,
How could you think I would tarry with you.'

Oh beautiful young girl and queenly maiden
Listen to my story and sit by my side,
For I'm not married and not a stranger
But a poor young fellow without esteem.
Come with me oh flower of womanhood:
Oh soft-lipped beauty be loving awhile,
And I'll be kissing my dearest darling
And playing you music for ever more.

Commercial recordings

Matt Cranitch has not, at the time of writing, recorded a solo album, but has played solos on the various albums recorded by Na Filí (*An Ghaoth Aniar (The West Wind)* — Mercier IRL9; *Farewell to Connacht* — Outlet SOLP 1010; *Na Filí 3* — Outlet SOLP 1017; *A Kindly Welcome* — Dolphin DOL 1008; *One Day for Recreation* — Circa 003). He has also played one track on a Comhaltas Ceoltóirí Eireann record *Fleá Cheoil*. The first tune noted here is not available on a commercial recording but 'Maidín Ró-mhoch', played by Matt, is available on the Na Filí LP *Chanters Tune* (Logo-Transatlantic TRA 353).

Index of names and titles

Number in bold type show the pages on which music notation of a tune or song appears.

English translations of Irish titles have only been indexed where the English version is itself a well known title.

For the convenience of non-Irish-speaking readers, titles beginning with the Irish articles 'An' and 'Na' are indexed under the letters A and N respectively.